THE OTHER HALF OF ASPERGER SYNDROME (AUTISM SPECTRUM DISORDER)

A Guide to Living in an Intimate Relationship with a Partner who is on the Autism Spectrum

2nd edition

MAXINE ASTON

Foreword by Tony Attwood

Jessica Kingsley *Publishers*
London and Philadelphia

This edition published in 2014
by Jessica Kingsley Publishers
73 Collier Street
London N1 9BE, UK
and
400 Market Street, Suite 400
Philadelphia, PA 19106, USA

www.jkp.com

First edition published in the United Kingdom in 2001
by The National Autistic Society, London

First edition published in the United States in 2001
by AAPC Publishing, Kansas

Copyright © Maxine Aston 2001, 2014
Foreword copyright © Tony Attwood 2014

Library of Congress Cataloging in Publication Data
Aston, Maxine C.
 The other half of Asperger syndrome (autism spectrum disorder) : a guide to living in an intimate
relationship with a partner who is on the autism spectrum / Maxine Aston ; foreword by Tony Attwood.
-- 2nd edition.
   pages cm
 Includes bibliographical references and index.
 ISBN 978-1-84905-498-0 (alk. paper)
 1. Asperger's syndrome--Patients--Family relationships. 2. Interpersonal relations. 3. Intimacy (Psychology) 4. Friendship. I. Attwood, Tony. II. Title.
 RC553.A88A799 2014
 616.85'8832--dc23
                    2013048195

British Library Cataloguing in Publication Data
A CIP catalogue record for this book is available from the British Library

ISBN 978 1 84905 498 0
eISBN 978 0 85700 920 3

Printed and bound in Great Britain

For all who love a partner who has
Asperger syndrome (Autism Spectrum Disorder)

CONTENTS

FOREWORD

In my clinical practice, I see many couples for advice on their relationship. They are often the parents of a child with an Autism Spectrum Disorder, recognising that one, or sometimes both, have the profile of abilities associated with Autism Spectrum Disorder, although expressed in a much more subtle way than in their child. I am now also seeing adults whom I originally saw as young children returning to the clinic for advice on how to maintain a successful relationship with their new partner. My clinic list also includes couples who have learnt about Asperger's syndrome (Autism Spectrum Disorder) from television programmes and films, and realised that the undiagnosed characteristics in one of the partners are affecting the relationship. Thus, there is an increasing need for literature and counselling for couples where one or both partners has undiagnosed or diagnosed Asperger's syndrome.

In 2001, Maxine wrote the first guide to living with a partner who has the characteristics of Asperger's syndrome. It was a slim volume, which was a reflection of the lack of knowledge at that time. We have learnt so much on relationships and Asperger's syndrome since 2001, and her seminal book needs to be revised. The second edition is also a slim volume, but the content is concise, clear and consistent with the latest clinical and research knowledge. This is an advantage, in that a small book is less daunting a prospect to read than a 'heavy' tome, and I want this book to be read by couples, and especially the partner who has the characteristics of Asperger's syndrome.

Maxine is an intrepid explorer of the world of relationships and Asperger's syndrome. This book is based on her professional experience over several decades as a relationship counsellor specialising in this area. She has also conducted research on this topic and written several books on relationships, as well as shared experiences, ideas and strategies with colleagues. She knows what she is talking about and her advice is very wise.

The second edition uses the same structure as the original book, but this edition has a greater depth of knowledge and more confidence and experience in the range of suggestions to improve the relationship, as well as more examples from her work with couples to illustrate specific points.

I consider that the partners of those who have Asperger's syndrome are quite remarkable people; this book is a tribute to their personal qualities and will contribute to a significant improvement in mutual understanding and enjoyment of the relationship.

Tony Attwood
Minds and Heart Clinic
Brisbane, Australia

ACKNOWLEDGEMENTS

I would like to thank all those who have helped in any way with the research and writing of this book.

In particular, I wish to thank all the courageous partners and couples who willingly allowed me to have an insight into their lives in the hope that their knowledge and experiences could help others; without them this book could not have been written. I would also like to thank Professor Tony Attwood, for giving me his valuable time by reading through the text and offering me his expert advice and opinions, and who has continued to do so over the years; Brenda Wall, who has the ability to move mountains and whose constant campaigning and determination have brought about many changes and helped create an awareness of the need for a book such as this; Dr Mark Forshaw, for his comments on the original text; Carol Darmon, for giving me suggestions and proofreading the text of the first edition; The National Autistic Society, whose staff have supported me throughout, especially Jan Snook, Chris Barson, Anne Cooper and David Potter; and Andrea Macleod, of the West Midlands Autistic Society, for her kind support. Last, but definitely not least, I wish to thank my three wonderful children, Zoe, Zara and William, for the strength and unselfish support that they have given me throughout my studies and the writing of the first and second edition of this book.

PREFACE

This book has been written as a guide to Asperger syndrome (Autism Spectrum Disorder) for anyone who has a partner with this condition, regardless of whether they are male, female, lesbian, gay or transgendered. The information used to compile this book has been drawn from three areas – my research into this specialised area, my work as a couples counsellor and my own personal experience, having lived with a partner who was given a diagnosis of Asperger syndrome.

This later second edition also draws from over a decade of experience of working with individuals, couples and families affected by Asperger syndrome. Since I wrote the first edition of this book, changes have been made to the most recent version of the *Diagnostic and Statistical Manual of Mental Disorders* (5th edition, APA 2013) and it has been decided by them no longer to use the term Asperger syndrome and to refer to individuals who come under this bracket as simply having an Autism Spectrum Disorder. This book maintains the use of the term Asperger syndrome to describe those at the higher-functioning end of this spectrum but it also acknowledges that those with Asperger syndrome fall under the broader term of Autism Spectrum Disorder. Whether your partner refers to themselves as having Asperger syndrome or an Autism Spectrum Disorder, the information in this book will be for you.

INTRODUCTION

It is over 13 years since The National Autistic Society contacted me and asked if I would write an information leaflet for partners who were in a relationship with an adult with Asperger syndrome. The leaflet rapidly grew into a book as I found there was so much information that I wanted to give.

Finding any research at the time was impossible, because there was none. I had already discovered during the course of my degree that there was simply nothing out there written about relationships. No one had ever researched into the area of couples when one partner was on the autism spectrum – many professionals still held the belief that people with Asperger syndrome did not marry or even form relationships. How wrong they were!

I managed to obtain 35 completed questionnaires from female partners of men with Asperger syndrome. In addition to this I was able to interview four adults with Asperger syndrome, three males and one female. The first edition was based on this research and my work as a couples counsellor.

Since 1998 I have specialised in counselling individuals, couples and families who are affected by Asperger syndrome (Autism Spectrum Disorder) and have worked with hundreds of clients. The one thing that has stayed consistent is the importance of acceptance, support and understanding which can make the difference between whether a couple stays together or not. The aim of this book is to offer a ray of hope to the non-Asperger partner and to offer them understanding and support in their endeavours to make sense of both their partner and their relationship.

The main body of this book has remained unchanged in this second edition. I have updated relevant information and also added information for men in relationships with Asperger women and those in gay, lesbian and transgendered relationships. I have also added short sections on denial, respect, sensory sensitivity and motherhood. This information was not available at the time of writing the first edition.

The Other Half of Asperger Syndrome was the first book written and published for partners in a relationship with someone on the autism spectrum ... its purpose remains the same, to offer hope.

PART I

The aim of the first part of this book is to provide some basic facts about Asperger syndrome (Autism Spectrum Disorder) and help those without it to understand this complex condition. I also attempt to offer some insight into what brings couples together in the first place and what may lead them to the realisation that Asperger syndrome may be present in one of the partners.

1

SOME FACTS ABOUT ASPERGER SYNDROME (AUTISM SPECTRUM DISORDER)

Hans Asperger and Asperger syndrome

In 1944, Hans Asperger (Asperger 1944) observed a pattern of behavioural problems in a group of boys while working in a Viennese clinic for disturbed children. He noted that these boys displayed an impairment in communication, both verbal and non-verbal. Their speech was inclined to be pedantic, sometimes repetitive and often quite one-sided, with lengthy accounts involving the child's favourite subject. Speech was often presented in a very monotonous or overly exaggerated way, with little facial expression; jokes could be misunderstood, as could the listener's responses. The group all had deficits in eye contact and body language. Asperger described the disorder as primarily a dysfunction in social interaction. He identified this condition as 'autistic psychopathy' and believed that it was an inherited personality disorder, as he recognised similar traits in the children's parents. The name Asperger Syndrome was first introduced by Lorna Wing in her classic paper published in 1981 (Wing 1981). She used the name Asperger syndrome in preference to 'autistic psychopathy'. The word 'psychopathy' means an abnormality of personality and implies sociopathic behaviour, a very different disorder from what we now think of as Asperger syndrome.

What is the autistic spectrum?

Asperger syndrome is an Autistic Spectrum Disorder. The autistic spectrum encompasses Asperger syndrome and autism, both of which may vary from severe to mild, or 'high-functioning'. Autism Spectrum Disorders are also referred to as pervasive developmental disorders.

There has been much debate as to whether or not there is a difference between high-functioning autism and Asperger syndrome, both among the professionals and for those on the spectrum. Much literature has been written on this subject (Schopler, Mesibov and Kunce 1998), and it is for each person to form their own opinions as to which name they feel is most appropriate for them.

Changes have now been made to the most recent version of the *Diagnostic and Statistical Manual of Mental Disorders* (5th edition, APA 2013) – it has been decided by the American Psychiatric Association (APA) to no longer use the term 'Asperger syndrome' but to refer to individuals who come under this bracket as simply having an 'Autism Spectrum Disorder'. Under the new diagnostic criteria those who were previously diagnosed with Asperger syndrome might fall under Autism Spectrum Disorder – Level 1.

What is Wing's triad of social and language impairments?

The three main criteria that people with Autism Spectrum Disorder share were arrived at by Lorna Wing and are now often referred to as Wing's triad of social and language impairments (Burgoine and Wing 1983). A diagnosis should be based on impairments in the following three areas:

- social relationships
- communication
- imagination

with a narrow, repetitive style regarding activities. There is a tendency to stick to very monotonous, fixed and seemingly dull thought patterns and behaviour.

However, to date, there is no specific universal agreement about the diagnostic criteria.

Is Asperger syndrome hereditary?

Hans Asperger, as we saw above, noticed that, among the children he diagnosed back in the 1940s, parents and their children had traits in common (Asperger 1944). Since then, evidence has been found for a genetic basis for Asperger syndrome, as in autism (Bailey *et al.* 1995). It has been suggested that genetic factors may play an even more important role in Asperger syndrome than in autism (Volkmar, Klin and Pauls 1998). There is still much uncertainty, though, as to which particular genes, and how many, are involved, and this has not changed since the writing of the first edition.

Studies indicate that more than one gene is responsible as the severity of autism can vary drastically, even among siblings – if only one or two genes were involved, the incidence in siblings would be much higher than it is (Folstein *et al.* 1998). It is more likely that there is a combination of genes that determine whether or not a child is born autistic. This would explain why not all family members are affected, and those who are will not always be affected to the same degree (Folstein *et al.* 1998; Folstein and Rosen-Sheidley 2001).

Another complication that hinders genetic research is that, in the case of autism, as with many other medical disorders, the parents often do not have another child following the birth of an autistic child, so families are small. It is therefore impossible to know if any subsequent children would also have been autistic (Folstein *et al.* 1998).

Some studies have measured whether or not children diagnosed as having Asperger syndrome have a parent who has Asperger syndrome or autistic traits. One study (Gillberg

1989) discovered that, in 57 per cent of cases of children with Asperger syndrome, there was a parent who displayed autistic traits or who also had Asperger syndrome. These figures do not tell us how likely it is that a couple where one partner has Asperger syndrome will have a child who will also have the syndrome. However, they do tell us that in 43 per cent of cases neither parent has Asperger syndrome. This further highlights just how complex the genetic factors involved in inheritance are, and might suggest that in some cases the possibility of an environmental cause should not be ruled out.

How common is it?

A study in Sweden in 1999 (Kadesjö, Gillberg and Hagberg 1999) found the prevalence figures for Asperger syndrome to be over 1 in 250. An earlier study in Sweden conducted by Ehlers and Gillberg in 1993 showed the prevalence figures to be approximately 1 in 300 children. It was also discovered in the study that approximately half of the sample of the children with Asperger syndrome had not been referred for diagnosis. This study indicated that there are probably many more cases of Asperger syndrome than we are currently aware of. Fear of discrimination has caused many adults to seek out an assessment privately and to rarely disclose the results beyond their immediate family. Based on this it would be impossible to even guess how many people are affected by Asperger syndrome.

More recent studies (Baird *et al.* 2006; Brugha *et al.* 2009, 2011, 2012) have been inclined to look at numbers of children or adults diagnosed with an Autism Spectrum Disorder that includes autism as well as Asperger syndrome, and these indicate that 1 in 100 individuals are on the autism spectrum.

2

IS ASPERGER SYNDROME (AUTISM SPECTRUM DISORDER) PREDOMINANTLY A MALE CONDITION?

Statistics report more males than females

Ehlers and Gillberg (1993) found that the male-to-female ratio was approximately 4:1. Clinical studies have concluded that it is much higher, suggesting ratios of between 10:1 and 15:1 (Ehlers and Gillberg 1993; Gillberg 1989; Wing 1981). These figures, however, are only based on the people who have received a formal diagnosis – naturally, they cannot account for those among the population who have not received a diagnosis.

A partner with Asperger syndrome may be male or female

During the course of my original research, I was only able to make contact with two women who have Asperger syndrome and who are in an intimate long-term relationship. This is likely to be due to the fact that, as we have seen, Asperger syndrome seems to affect more males than females (Ehlers and Gillberg 1993; Gillberg 1989; Wing 1981).

In my own work I am seeing more and more women with Asperger syndrome, and am of the opinion that there are far more women on the spectrum than statistics suggest. Women with Asperger syndrome are often excellent at learning social skills, and many have the ability to disguise their social difficulties.

Why are females less likely to be detected?

Tony Attwood described women with Asperger syndrome as being particularly good at imitating the social actions of others and more likely to be described as immature than 'odd' (Attwood 1998). This would enable a woman with Asperger syndrome to be able to learn appropriate behaviours, coping skills and strategies to deal with social situations. However, this can come at a great cost to their own well-being, causing both stress and anxiety.

The majority of the books that have been written by adults with Asperger syndrome have been written by women. This may mean that women with the syndrome are more concerned about being heard and are better able to express themselves in literature than men with the syndrome, and that they wish to be acknowledged by all who care to read their valuable accounts of living with Asperger syndrome. One book in particular that highlights a woman's ability to remain undetected is by Liane Holliday Willey, *Pretending To Be Normal* (Holliday Willey 1999). It offers an insider's view into being a wife and a mother with Asperger syndrome. A male reader who suspects or knows that his female partner has Asperger syndrome may gain much valuable information from reading this book. Another more recent book that offers valuable information on the experience of being a female with Asperger syndrome is *Aspergirls* by Rudy Simone (2010).

Does gender make a difference to any problems in a relationship?

The core problems that Asperger syndrome creates for the individual are the same for women as they are for men, so most of the information given in this book applies to both sexes. The extent to which a particular individual is affected and how they deal with the problems that having Asperger syndrome can cause, however, varies between males and females. This can be explained by the fact that Asperger syndrome seems to exaggerate some of the difficulties that some men may already have with verbal and non-verbal communication.

It has been claimed that women are more adept than men at interpreting non-verbal information (Golan, Baron-Cohen and Hill 2006; Montagne *et al.* 2005; Noller 1980), which may give women an automatic advantage in the area of social skills and communication. It is therefore possible for a woman with Asperger syndrome to have a greater ability to conceal the emotional and social problems she may be experiencing in her everyday life than a man with the syndrome. The advantages that women have regarding social skills could make it harder to detect Asperger syndrome in the more able woman, and if she has learned good social strategies and coping skills, her partner may remain unaware of its presence. He may even find the lack of emotion an advantage in their relationship, especially if they share the same special interest. This, however, is not always the case.

When the other half is male

In her interview with Professor Tony Attwood, Liane Holliday Willey describes her relationship with her husband as 'a breeze' (Holliday Willey and Attwood 2000). One reason she gives for this is the similarities between them, with regards to Asperger traits. Having now worked with a number of couples, when it is the female who has Asperger syndrome it has become apparent to me that the majority of women I see choose men who are also on the spectrum. The men they choose would be more likely to come under the heading of 'traits of Asperger's', however, and many would be unlikely to meet the full criteria for Asperger syndrome.

The reasoning behind this seems to be that women are more likely to choose a partner to whom they can relate whereas men are more likely to choose a partner who compensates for what they find difficult or cannot do. My experience certainly backs this up, although this does not suggest it is always easy for the man who is the partner of a female with Asperger syndrome. He may well struggle with making sense of her reactions to him or her need for control in the relationship. He will find himself feeling just as confused as a woman in the same place; the problem is he is less likely to seek help or to discuss it with his friends.

What about gay, lesbian and transgendered relationships?

Since the time of my original research I have worked with gay, lesbian and transgendered relationships and have found that in the majority of cases the issues that arise between them are no different than those with heterosexual couples. The pattern that the non-Asperger syndrome partner is very nurturing, sociable and emotional appears to be repeated in the relationship.

I have not yet encountered a gay, lesbian or transgendered couple where both were on the spectrum; perhaps it is the case that same-sex relationships where both are on the spectrum are relatively successful and there is no need to seek out counselling services. Sharing the same gender, whether or not Asperger syndrome is relevant, removes the issues that can be caused by gender difference. In addition it appears that in the case of two men, when one had Asperger syndrome there was often a high level of acceptance, understanding and capacity to work at the relationship shared between them. This could suggest that sharing the same gender, when both male, lessens the impact of issues caused by lack of emotional reciprocity.

Why the apparent increase in the numbers of men and women with Asperger syndrome?

Why does it seem that more men and women are now being diagnosed as having Asperger syndrome? Besides the obvious reason that awareness of Asperger syndrome has increased greatly over the past three decades, making it more likely that if you have the syndrome this will be recognised, there does appear to be a gender difference between men and women as to how they become aware they might be on the spectrum. With regard to men it is more likely it is their partner who recognises they might be on the spectrum. A reason for this may be that, in the past, the behaviour of men with Asperger syndrome was more likely to be overlooked than it is today. The more able men with the syndrome who do seek out relationships are often very hard and conscientious workers, so they are often also good providers. In view of these dispositions, their problems with social interaction may have been conveniently overlooked in the past, as the financial support offered by these men was possibly considered more important to their partners then than how they related to them on an emotional level.

Today, however, women are asking for better emotional interaction and a deeper level of communication with their partners. They are no longer prepared to accept the 'women feel and men think' view. Most women expect understanding, intimacy and emotional support from their partner; they want to be able to express their feelings and to be understood.

Equally, the financial status of women in society is changing rapidly, with employers recognising women's potential in terms of careers and increasing flexibility in the job market. With the rise in the numbers of jobs available to women and the increase in women's capacity to earn, the traditional dependence on a man as the sole financial supporter has, for some women, decreased. As women become more independent, they ask for support in more areas than just the financial side of the relationship. Most women want more from their partners than just money; they want to feel loved and appreciated.

All these factors may explain why more men with Asperger syndrome are being identified today. Women are not keeping quiet and they are recognising that their partners are not simply behaving 'just like a man'. Thus, the numbers of men with Asperger syndrome may simply have increased because their problems with social interaction are no longer being sidelined.

This is quite different from the women who seek out an assessment. Women seem more likely to be aware of the difficulties they encounter in friendships and relationships and often discover Asperger syndrome for themselves and decide to explore the possibility that they may or may not be on the spectrum.

3

SUSPECTED, UNDIAGNOSED ASPERGER SYNDROME (AUTISM SPECTRUM DISORDER)

The first step

In my original research I received almost three times as many replies from respondents who strongly suspected their partner had Asperger syndrome than I did from those with a partner who had been diagnosed. The journey of discovery for those who are uncertain as to whether or not their partner has it can be confusing and sometimes ambiguous. One of the aims of this book is to offer some guidance and attempt to clarify some of the doubts that you may have if you are in this situation.

There are various reasons that might lead you to wonder if your partner has Asperger syndrome. Asperger syndrome is being mentioned more and more in the media and so knowing about it may lead you to think that your partner could have the syndrome. Alternatively, you might have a child who has been diagnosed as having Asperger syndrome or autism. Such awareness of autistic spectrum conditions may provoke the realisation that there are similarities between your child's behaviour and your partner's. Equally, if you are an adult with undiagnosed Asperger syndrome, you may even recognise for yourself that you have problems in the same areas as your child.

The paradoxical nature of Asperger syndrome

A person living with a partner who has Asperger syndrome may have been aware for many years that something is not quite right, and perhaps have a sense of something being missing or not fitting into place. Someone who is in a sexual and intimate relationship with another is more likely than anyone else to know the person on a very intimate and personal level. They will be very aware of what a paradox their partner is: so capable in some areas, yet so disabled in others. They will also be aware that their partner is unable to understand what it is they do, or fails to do, that can cause both themselves and their partner so many problems and misunderstandings.

Asperger syndrome can make a more capable high achiever seem just such a paradox. It can give many mixed and ambiguous messages that may lead to a lot of confused emotions for partners living with them.

A person with Asperger syndrome may be an expert in a particular, often obscure, field – Edwardian architecture, computers, feminism, aircraft, automobiles, theology, music or something perhaps more bizarre such as the shapes of electric pylons or empty cleaning cartons. They will know their chosen field of interest inside out. Their rote memory can be amazing and their ability to recall facts and figures will defy all logic, especially as they often seem to acquire all this knowledge without any effort. They may be able to do all these things and often be very competent at them, and yet the non-Asperger syndrome partner may express that they have not felt able to leave their partner in charge of the children, or to attend a social gathering, for fear that there would be some unpredicted crisis and their partner would have difficulty coping with it.

4

OBSESSIVE BEHAVIOUR OR SPECIAL INTERESTS?

Routines can be rigid and precise

A person with Asperger syndrome (Autism Spectrum Disorder) may have many rigid daily routines, and it may have been these that first made their partner notice that this was not usual behaviour, not something you would expect a person to engage in. It could be that mealtimes have to be very precise, always served at the same time every day, and certain foods have to be cooked in a certain way. Many different routines have been identified in adults with Asperger syndrome, and how closely these have to be observed will vary from person to person. When a routine has become firmly established, everyone will have to fit in with it; any form of change is likely to cause mayhem. This fixed regime can make something quite simple, like going out for a meal, hard work and certainly not the enjoyable experience it should be.

These strict routines can include door and window locking, turning off the gas, mealtimes, only eating certain foods, only using certain cleaning materials, taking certain routes in the car and many more. You might have thought initially that your partner was just being awkward, but there is a chance that, before Asperger syndrome was suspected, the behaviour may have been attributed to a condition called obsessive compulsive disorder (OCD).

Asperger syndrome and obsessive compulsive disorder

OCD can often manifest itself in the form of repetitive behaviours similar to those already described. Obsessions with cleaning and checking have been identified in cases of Asperger syndrome and these can be easily confused with OCD when there is not a full awareness of the diagnostic criteria for Asperger syndrome. In some cases, OCD can occur independently in someone who has Asperger syndrome, and this would be for a psychologist or psychiatrist to assess. They are certainly not the same thing, however.

More to Asperger syndrome than just obsessions

Asperger syndrome does not end there – it is not just about having obsessions or routines, and some people with Asperger syndrome do not have strong obsessions or routines. To receive a diagnosis of Asperger syndrome requires that other areas of life are also affected. Those with the syndrome will have problems with communication and it may be difficult for them to engage in a very deep, meaningful conversation about their partner's feelings and how those feelings affect the relationship. They will have problems in reading non-verbal signals, such as facial expressions and body language, and also in being able to give the right responses when talking. Many men and women have said that they 'did not feel necessary' to their Asperger partners on an emotional level, and that they were needed more for what they did than for who they were and how they felt.

Not just a case of men being men

If your partner with Asperger syndrome is male, some may argue that this is just the way some men are and that women have always been better empathisers than men. Asperger syndrome, however, is something very different, and partners may sense that this is not just a case of their partners being 'typical men'.

You may also sense that there is a deeper problem than your partner just being awkward because something about his responses and actions shows that he is uncertain about what to do or how you are expecting him to respond. This may lead you to think at times that it is you who are unable to make yourself understood, and that the problem in communicating lies with you.

Questioning your sanity

Many women and men have reported that they felt they were going completely mad. They could not understand why their Asperger partners were unable to comprehend what they were trying to tell them, and why they would accuse them of criticising every time they tried to help or offer some advice. Some non-Asperger partners felt they were becoming 'nags' because they ended up repeating the same things over and over again, finding themselves in the same locked situation with their partners.

Can things change? The answer is 'yes'. However, without knowledge of Asperger syndrome, it may be you who have to do most of the changing. Some non-Asperger partners initially reported that they tried to suppress what they felt in order to deal with what their partners were doing in a less emotional way. They tried to avoid certain situations and topics, especially those involving some sort of social interaction.

5

SOCIALISING, FRIENDS, PRESENT AND PAST

Social situations

There is the strong possibility that social situations involving both partners in a couple will have, in some instances, become embarrassing or highly stressful. One woman described visiting the local supermarket with her partner for their weekly shopping. She reported the feelings of utter embarrassment she experienced when her partner insisted on lining up all the cans on the conveyor belt in a precise symmetrical way, completely oblivious to the long queue of impatient shoppers forming behind them.

A couple I counselled recalled how when hosting a party his partner left half way through and took the dog for a walk; this would have been okay if he had returned before the party finished. Even worse was the experience of a man who described how he had arranged a surprise party for his Asperger wife's fortieth birthday. He went to great lengths to keep it secret and pretended they were going out for a quiet meal together. He arranged for all their friends and family to be in the agreed place and to sing 'Happy Birthday' when they made their entrance. He could only look on in embarrassment when his wife went into complete meltdown and ran out of the room. It took him over half an hour to persuade her to come out of the ladies' toilet. He learned from this that surprises were not a good idea for someone on the spectrum.

The bluntness and honesty of the Asperger partner can also cause problems in social activities. For example, one woman described the feeling of horror she felt when a friend asked her what she thought of her new outfit. Her partner, who was standing with her, answered instead and gave her his honest opinion. He also recommended that if she lost a few pounds the outfit would look better!!

Friends

The behaviour of a person with Asperger syndrome (Autism Spectrum Disorder) may at times appear rude, especially to those who are not aware of the syndrome. So it may not come as too much of a surprise to find that a person with the syndrome does not always have any close or long-term friends. What may be surprising, however, is that they seem never to have had any close friends, and do not appear to have really needed any.

There may be different reasons for the lack of friends. One may be that they simply never wanted any and were always too absorbed in some hobby, or simply chose very solitary pursuits. In the case of more able partners with Asperger syndrome, it is more likely that they have always wanted friends – probably quite desperately at times – and may have wondered why, whenever they tried to make friends, they never seemed to get it quite right. Some may have tried taking on different personas to try and fit in with peer groups. The problems with forming friendships go right back to childhood.

Asperger syndrome is for life

Asperger syndrome is present from birth – it is not something that develops in later life and it will not go away. It is not the result of childhood or adult trauma, nor is it the result of abuse or emotional neglect or rejection by parents who could not express their emotions.

It is not always detected in the early years and may even go unrecognised until adolescence or adulthood. Adolescence is often a very bewildering and intensely traumatic time for those with Asperger syndrome. It can leave them feeling that they were treated quite unfairly as a child and teenager, especially if, like many children with Asperger syndrome, they were bullied at school.

The effect of childhood bullying and Asperger syndrome

Bullying can have an adverse effect on all children. It can lower their self-esteem, confidence and ability to be assertive. To children with Asperger syndrome, bullying may often go unreported and undetected, and the lessons it teaches about other people can live with them all their lives. They may carry with them the belief that others are out to trick them, to make fun of them and make them look stupid. This may exaggerate their reaction to perceived criticisms of themselves, and it is this heightened sensitivity that partners may experience first-hand when trying to discuss how they feel about a particular issue.

6

TRYING TO COMMUNICATE

Taking things literally

Problems with literal and double meanings can cause many misunderstandings for those with Asperger syndrome (Autism Spectrum Disorder), many of whom complain that they wish people would just say what they mean.

In a couple where one partner has not yet been diagnosed as having Asperger syndrome, the non-Asperger partner can feel quite bewildered and at times infuriated that their partner cannot understand what they are trying to say and often seems to completely miss the point. Some say that they do not see why something so simple should cause such chaos. One woman explained how she had told her Asperger husband she would 'kill him' if he forgot to pick up the dry cleaning in his lunch hour. She was going to speak at an important conference that evening and needed the outfit that was at the dry cleaners. He forgot to collect it and took her threat to kill him quite seriously, so he was too afraid to go home. She eventually received a call from her sister-in-law to say that he had phoned her because he was concerned that if he returned home he was in danger of losing his life.

As well as misunderstandings over the literal meanings in communication, non-verbal communication between partners may also cause problems.

Giving non-verbal messages

It can be difficult for those with Asperger syndrome to get facial expressions right, and knowing when to smile can be one problem. You may be telling your partner something quite serious and important, but when you glance at them they are smiling, leaving you thinking, 'What are they smiling about?'

Eye movements may also appear odd, your partner perhaps staring for too long or looking away at an inappropriate moment. This lack of coordination with others' facial expressions can also show itself in body language.

Body language and personal space

Some with Asperger syndrome do not have the natural ability to learn the unwritten rules regarding personal space that others take for granted. They will sometimes stand where they want to stand and seem unaware that they may be standing too close to someone. This may give out strange and sometimes threatening signals to someone who is not aware of the reasons behind this behaviour.

Hand movements may sometimes be non-existent or exaggerated. People with Asperger syndrome may walk in a slightly odd way: their movements might be quite stiff, their arms swinging in a kind of regimented way, or perhaps there might be a clumsiness to their movements. There may also be an awkwardness or oddness to the way in which they take part in conversations. Some partners describe their facial expressions as 'wooden'. Eye contact can be evasive and this may sometimes give the impression that there is a lack of honesty or openness, which is not the case. When you know that someone has Asperger syndrome, these problematic issues in communication can be explained and understood.

7

SEEKING A DIAGNOSIS

Making the decision to be assessed

A couple needs to give very careful consideration to the question of whether or not they should seek out a diagnosis.

If one partner does not want to accept or investigate the possibility of Asperger syndrome (Autism Spectrum Disorder), the other partner has to decide how important it is to them, and if they can live without having a formal diagnosis. Whatever they decide, it must be the decision of the person who may have Asperger syndrome to go and seek a referral, and the other partner should not try to force the situation either way. This decision should be reached in the other partner's own time, when they are ready to face it, and feel prepared and willing to accept a possible positive diagnosis. After all, it is no small thing to face the possibility of finding out that they have a lifelong disorder that cannot be cured.

On the positive side, receiving a diagnosis can offer the opportunity for the person to learn specific skills and make improvements in their personal and professional life.

The importance of being aware

Having a diagnosis can make a great deal of difference to the couple's relationship as it brings an awareness of the effects of Asperger syndrome on the couple. Awareness, followed by acceptance, is the first step towards dealing with them effectively.

Even if the adult who may have Asperger syndrome does not wish to go for an assessment, as long as they are aware and accept that it may be the cause of some of their problems, the couple will be able to move forward and work on the difficulties they are facing. If, however, the partner who may have Asperger syndrome is unwilling to accept that they may be on the spectrum and blames everything or everyone else for the problems in the relationship, then it will be very difficult for the relationship to survive. Sometimes the blame can be directed at the partner without Asperger syndrome, and this can have a devastating effect on both them and the relationship.

Asperger syndrome in denial

It may be the case that the partner with Asperger syndrome refuses to seek a diagnosis and completely refutes the idea that they might be on the spectrum. Living with a partner in denial is the hardest thing of all, regardless of whether they are male or female. If a partner has Asperger syndrome and refuses to accept or explore the idea, the chances are that they will often blame their partner for the misunderstandings that occur in the relationship. This blame will add to the confusion and low self-esteem the non-Asperger partner may already be experiencing, and they will have to decide for themselves whether the cost to them is too high to continue in the relationship.

Seeking a referral

If a couple decides to seek a referral, this can be done by both partners visiting their GP and discussing it, or if they can afford it, private advice. If at all possible it is important for the couple to check that the clinician to whom they are referred is informed about or specialises in Asperger syndrome. Although professionals are becoming more knowledgeable in this area, there are still many who do not yet fully understand what having Asperger syndrome implies, and how to recognise and diagnose it correctly.

Medical health workers sometimes link Asperger syndrome with severe autism, and have very misguided and preconceived ideas about what being on the autism spectrum entails.

One myth, for instance, is that adults with Asperger syndrome do not form sexual relationships or marry, which is clearly not the case.

It is helpful for couples to go together to see their GP as the partner without Asperger syndrome may be able to provide valuable information and give the other partner support. Just a short consultation with a GP will not be enough to enable the GP to make a decision as to whether or not one partner has Asperger syndrome, so a referral for a full assessment should be offered.

Coming to a diagnosis

Different clinicians may use various methods to arrive at a diagnosis. It is very helpful if both partners go to the appointment together as the more information that can be provided the better, especially any details about the developmental history of the person with suspected Asperger syndrome. These last details are very important to help form an accurate diagnosis, and questions will be asked about childhood, parents and siblings, any problems at work, adolescence, friendships and relationships. Information about hobbies, special interests and routines will also be asked for, as well as life within the family and any other particular areas that may be problematic.

A positive diagnosis

If a couple has reached the stage of a consultation, it is very possible that there will be a positive diagnosis of Asperger syndrome. However prepared you both are for being told that one of you has Asperger syndrome, it will almost always have an impact. You may feel relieved initially or completely numb.

The partner with Asperger syndrome, on the other hand, could appear completely unaffected. One woman described how her partner was more impressed by the fact the psychiatrist had the same tie on as he did than being told that he had Asperger syndrome. It is therefore important not to presume that a partner will feel unduly disturbed or horrified by the diagnosis. It is also a good idea for each partner in a couple to say how they feel about the diagnosis and not to make any assumptions for each other.

8

AFTER THE DIAGNOSIS, WHAT NEXT?

Acceptance

After receiving a diagnosis of Asperger syndrome (Autism Spectrum Disorder), give yourselves time to accept it. Although for some it may seem unfair or a hopeless situation on discovering for certain that their partner has Asperger syndrome, it can also come as quite a revelation. It may help to make sense of many of the things that were hard to understand about a partner's behaviour, and explain some of the problems that have hindered the relationship.

Once you know that Asperger syndrome has been responsible for some of the problems you have been having, you can extend your knowledge and understanding of the disorder, and work out better strategies for dealing with these problematic areas. There is no cure for Asperger syndrome, however, no magic pill or remedy to put it right, and a lot of hard work and changes will be required by both partners, but especially by the partner without Asperger syndrome.

You will both have to decide whom you are going to tell and how to explain what Asperger syndrome is. Some may find it difficult to understand or accept. Others may, wrongfully, view it as a mental illness and be fearful, thinking that it makes your partner odd or different, someone to be wary of. It is important that whoever is told receives an adequate explanation of what Asperger syndrome is. To help others understand it may be useful to tell them that it is a difference in the neurological wiring of the brain. Use the example of dyslexia as a comparison, explaining that rather than affecting reading, writing and spelling, Asperger syndrome causes difficulty in other specific areas, such as social interaction and communication, verbal and non-verbal, empathetic thought and possibly obsessive tendencies and a need for routine. Beyond these areas your partner is capable and no different from anyone else. The main thing is that your partner should be treated with the same amount of respect and dignity as any other human being.

The end of the journey to discovery

After receiving a diagnosis, as the partner without Asperger syndrome you may be left feeling both happy and sad. Although you are likely to feel a sense of relief and that you now have the ability to understand what has been causing many of the problems in the relationship, you may also feel like you have reached the end of a journey and be rather exhausted by it all.

You will very likely be in need of some comforting. The trouble is that your partner may not be aware of this need or be able to offer this kind of support and warmth. Tell your partner how you feel, but not in a judgmental way: this is not about blame. Explain in a direct and clear way that you are relieved you now both know the reason why there have been some problems in the relationship and that together you can now work at sorting things out. If possible, do this when you are both sitting quietly together, have plenty of time and will not be interrupted.

One woman I spoke to had an agreement with her husband that, rather than expecting him automatically to know, she would always tell him when she wanted a hug. This took the pressure away from him and he was always happy to oblige. If your partner, though, is not able to offer any comfort, then it is important to seek support from friends and family who can prove quite invaluable at this time.

Feelings of loss

There may be a sense of loss at this time, almost a feeling that something has died. This is not surprising – something *has* died.

The relationship as it was perceived before the diagnosis is no more, and you now know that things will never be quite the same again.

You know that all the tactics and ways that have been used to try and change things in the past have been ineffective and you will have to start all over again with new ones.

You may feel that you no longer know the person you fell in love with.

For all these and other reasons, it is often the partner without Asperger syndrome who is left with a sense of loss. This time can feel quite lonely as it is unlikely that your partner will be able to empathise with you or share these feelings.

Feelings of anger

Sometimes there can be a feeling of anger once a diagnosis of Asperger syndrome has been accepted for your partner. You may feel you have been cheated out of having a 'normal' relationship or that you have spent years trying to achieve something that was never going to be possible.

The feelings of anger may not be directed at anybody in particular but may be aimed at your partner's parents, life, God, the professionals or something else. You may feel the need for a scapegoat and so your anger may be directed at your partner, despite the fact that it is not their fault they have Asperger syndrome. This can be disruptive and negative for both of you.

In time, the anger will burn out. Only then should you start to make decisions about what to do and where to go from there. Rash decisions made while you are still in the middle of this angry phase will be short-lived and probably quite negative, so it is important to take things easy until the anger subsides.

Where to go from here

Some men and women report feeling like they should get out altogether and start a new life. If you do decide to do this, it is important that you do not feel like a deserter who has abandoned a sinking ship. Not everybody can live with the absence of intimate communication, reciprocated feelings and empathy that, to a greater or lesser extent, are part of Asperger syndrome.

Before the diagnosis, which brings with it the realisation that Asperger syndrome is the cause of some of the problems, you may have kept struggling to bring about changes in the relationship and lived in the hope that things could and would change. Hope keeps people going through many adverse situations. With a diagnosis or acceptance that a partner has Asperger syndrome, however, that hope might feel as if it has been wiped out. This does not have to be the case – your goals just have to become realistic. Indeed, many relationships where one partner has Asperger syndrome are successful.

Hope can live on

If you are the partner without Asperger syndrome, a diagnosis gives you two positive pieces of information:

- you now know that you are not going crazy

- your partner did not mean to upset you by some of the things they did or did not do.

Men and women report many instances that they had found hurtful before receiving a positive diagnosis, such as a birthday card signed like a business letter, not being visited in hospital by their partner because hospitals make them feel uneasy, being abandoned at a party or feeling let down by their partner's reluctance to share in an intimate moment. Often they have found that, afterwards, they are able to understand some of these things that had previously left them feeling upset or bewildered. One man in particular described how knowing his wife had Asperger syndrome helped him make sense of her behaviour. He had thought she did not care for him and only thought of her own needs; discovering Asperger syndrome changed his perception and saved their marriage. Things that had happened that they could not understand before started to make sense and fall into place.

Some men and women, though, were left wondering why they had not realised earlier what was causing the problems and why they had turned a blind eye to the obvious fact that this was not just selfish or awkward behaviour by their partner, that there was something more at work. The next chapter sets out to explain why some of these signs are unconsciously ignored, and what it is that attracted you to your partner in the first place.

9

INITIAL ATTRACTION

Kind, gentle men

This chapter is written for women and men who have a male partner with Asperger syndrome (Autism Spectrum Disorder), as I do not have sufficient data regarding what attracts men to women who have the syndrome. However, it appears likely from the information I do have that a woman with Asperger syndrome will seek out someone who is likely to be a reliable and steady father figure, does not make strong emotional or intimate demands on her, and allows her a lot of freedom and autonomy in the relationship. This, for many non-Asperger men, can hold much appeal.

Most of the women with male partners with the syndrome describe them as being very kind, gentle and quiet men when they first met them, and these were the characteristics that they were initially attracted to. These men tended to display a naiveté that had a boyish essence to it, and the women they often chose had strong maternal, caring and warm ways. So almost instantly there can be a 'fit' between the two halves of a couple of this type.

The feminine side of men with Asperger syndrome

Boys with Asperger syndrome are sometimes teased at school because they adopt a somewhat feminine approach, and are less likely to conform to social stereotypes of masculine and feminine behaviour than is the case with their peers. Their mothers are more likely to be their role models than their fathers, because it is often their mothers they spend more time with. This could lead to boys displaying mannerisms and gestures that could be misinterpreted by other children as being 'girlish'; name-calling and bullying could be the consequence.

Such a feminine side in an adult male can be very appealing to some women, however. Many men with Asperger syndrome are quite happy to cook, clean, iron and even arrange flowers if they so wish. They do not feel obligated to fulfil and display masculine roles, but are much more likely to do what pleases them, rather than what society states they are supposed to do. They may have quite a gentle approach and rarely display aggressive behaviour. Many women interpret this as meaning that they are sure enough of their masculinity to be in touch with their feminine side, and see this as a positive quality in a partner.

As men with Asperger syndrome often choose women who are quite strong, independent and nurturing, this all fits together very well, for a while. It is only after a time together that the contradiction of this feminine side emerges. Although the man may be gentle, they may also begin to display some rather chauvinistic traits. A chosen partner may be expected to fill a certain role and that role may depend on the man's mother. He may expect things done for him exactly as his mother did for him. It is possible that he chose his partner because she was in some way like his mother, and there is a possibility that the man's partner may be older than he is.

An older woman

It is not the case that men with Asperger syndrome deliberately search out older partners. However, many of the non-Asperger women I encountered in the course of my research were older than their partners. This finding differs from most of the existing literature on couples, which indicates that it is far more likely that the male will be older than the female.

One of the theories proposed to explain this is that a man will exchange his wealth for a woman's youth and attractiveness. This rule does not seem to apply when the man in a relationship has Asperger syndrome, and this can feel very flattering for a woman living in a society where youth and looks seem to govern so many men's choices of female partners. It may be that age is not too important to someone who has Asperger syndrome, as they often appear not to discriminate on the basis of a person's age or status. It may also be that men with Asperger syndrome prefer, and feel more comfortable with, an older woman, and have decided that age equates to maternal and nurturing ways.

Since the time of my original research I have found that a woman with Asperger syndrome is also likely to choose a man who is much older. Sometimes this can be 20 or more years. I believe the reasons for this are very similar to men with Asperger syndrome, and often the woman may be seeking out a man who is a father figure and who will take care of her needs. This is very flattering for the non-Asperger male.

Hard workers and good providers

Focusing again on couples when the Asperger partner is male, another reason for attraction may be that the more able men with Asperger syndrome are often highly qualified and have very well-paid jobs – frequently within the fields of engineering, science, mathematics or computing. The ability to work with objects rather than people could be described as a characteristic trait of Asperger syndrome.

Simon Baron-Cohen described individuals with Asperger syndrome as being highly capable in the area of 'folk physics', which is understanding objects, and quite poor in the area of 'folk psychology' (Baron-Cohen and Wheelwright 1999), which is understanding people and their thoughts. Thus, unfortunately, when they have to deal with other people – whether it is management, other employees or the public – they can face major problems, unless they are fortunate enough to work in very liberal surroundings or solitary conditions. However, some employers will often overlook the social problems an adult with the syndrome displays as their hard and conscientious work compensates for it.

Interests in common

There may be similar interests or a particular hobby shared by the couple. Love of the theatre, politics, religion, and, in particular, music were all mentioned as shared common interests that brought a couple together.

Sometimes, though, the special interest is not always as straightforward as it might first appear. One woman reported that she had been attracted to her husband because of his Christian beliefs. He said he was interested in the Bible, but you can imagine her surprise when he proudly showed her his collection of hundreds of bibles. Another woman was pleased to have found someone who shared her interest in classical music. In fact, her new partner seemed quite an expert on the composers – so much so that she eventually realised this was his one and only topic of conversation. As long as they discussed music and composers, things were fine, but beyond that it was as though he had absolutely nothing to say to her. Music was his obsession.

Obsessive love

Women and men have reported that they eventually realised that *they* were their partner's obsession a little while after they started seeing each other. It would be difficult for most people not to feel flattered by so much attention and devotion from someone just wanting to please them and spend all their time with them. It is no wonder that many men and women feel important, special and needed at this time.

Most people want to feel needed, but there is a difference between being needed and totally depended on, which is what this need can gradually become. It is this obsessive love, appealing and attractive in the beginning, that eventually becomes the very thing that drives the two people in the relationship apart.

Some are left feeling like the responsibility for the whole relationship is weighing on their shoulders.

Whirlwind romance

Some men and women talked about having gone through quite a short, whirlwind romance that moved rapidly through the stages of courtship and on to marriage. Courtship with men and women with Asperger syndrome may be short-lived if their sole desire is to find a partner. It is often a need to be married that motivates men and women with Asperger syndrome to seek out a partner in the first place. If they believe they have found a suitable partner who has all the qualities they are looking for, then the topic of marriage or a civil partnership may enter the conversation quite early on.

Love is blind

'Love is blind', they say, and this is especially true of the early stages of a relationship. It is not uncommon to focus on and exaggerate a new-found partner's positive qualities. Non-Asperger women can think, 'Here is this caring and (possibly) handsome man, with a good, respectable, well-paid job, who is honest, kind and gentle – I'm so lucky.' In the case of non-Asperger men they are often very flattered by the woman's intense attraction to him, and in many cases she will be much younger and may take more care of how she looks. He will be very proud to show her off to his friends and family.

Both non-Asperger men and women may ignore the fact that their friends or family find their new partners a little bit eccentric or different, or that misunderstandings and communication problems are occurring.

Some men and women turn a blind eye when, for instance, their partner insists on being in charge of planning all their outings or journeys, sometimes in great detail. One woman described how her husband even insisted on teaching her the 'correct way' of putting the rubbish in the bin. Equally a man described how he simply accepted his partner's insistence that she liked to wear sunglasses when they went into any well-lit restaurant or bar. In the early days of the relationship, many men and women decide they can live with these unusual little ways, but it can become increasingly difficult to do so as time goes on.

After the honeymoon period

Some men and women talked about feeling that, once they were married or in a civil partnership, their partner stopped trying – the romance ended as did the feeling of being important and special to their partner. Some felt that their partner's efforts to please them suddenly stopped and they simply returned to their former lifestyle – they found themselves being expected to fit in with all their partner's needs for routine and a schedule, to tolerate their special interests and not have a social life, intimate communication and, in some cases, a sexual relationship.

Fulfilling a need

Some men and women described this time as particularly difficult as they tried to understand their Asperger partner's needs. They did not want to give up and walk out and, when talking failed, many tried to change themselves and began to question their own sanity. Some described it as feeling like they were not being appreciated for who they were and, no matter how hard they tried, communication constantly broke down. They felt themselves getting more and more angry and frustrated as they tried to make sense of things and understand just what it was that somehow kept leading them back to the same place. Some talked about having a feeling that something was missing, like the last piece needed to complete a jigsaw, and the sense that they were there simply to fulfil their partner's needs rather than there being the necessary give-and-take in a relationship.

Being stuck in this very painful situation and feeling bewildered and confused may sometimes go on for months or, in many cases, years before the couple discovers what is wrong. Some women reported going to their doctor and being recommended for couples counselling, or sometimes the couples arranged to go for counselling themselves. This is an avenue many couples find themselves travelling down when one of the partners has Asperger syndrome.

10

GETTING HELP

Couples counselling

Receiving couples counselling when relationships have run into problems can, in many cases, help revive them. Indeed, the problems in many marriages and relationships have been solved within a counselling room. Unfortunately, this does not often appear to be the case when one partner has Asperger syndrome (Autism Spectrum Disorder).

For some, the result may be disastrous, leaving the partner who does not have Asperger syndrome feeling unheard, frustrated and very angry. The reason for this is likely to be that the presence of Asperger syndrome has not been recognised by either the couple or the counsellor. However, from my own work as a couples counsellor, I know that this need not be the case.

When there is an awareness that one of the couple has Asperger syndrome and the counsellor is experienced in this area, counselling can be a very positive and rewarding experience for both partners. Couples have been able to achieve many successful changes by using suitable coping skills and strategies. Counselling can help sift through the problem areas and identify what is due to the partner having Asperger syndrome and what is not. The result is that the couple feels better equipped to deal with problems, and each feels more appreciated and understood by the other. The couple feels listened to, validated and supported in their attempts to maintain and strengthen the relationship, which means a lot. When a couple seeks counselling, it is quite possible that neither partner knows that one of them has Asperger syndrome. This alone can mean that counselling will not work. If, at a later date, one of them receives a positive diagnosis, the counsellor may be held responsible by the couple for not knowing at the time that this was the problem and acting on it. However, counsellors are not psychologists, nor are they psychiatrists, so they are unlikely to have been trained to recognise a complex condition such as Asperger syndrome. Nor are counsellors qualified to make an official diagnosis; they should, though, have enough knowledge about Asperger syndrome to be able to refer or signpost the couple in the right direction.

If counsellors suspect that clients have Asperger syndrome, they may suggest that the couple contacts The National Autistic Society and seek further information for themselves. Alternatively, they may be advised to both visit their GP together to seek a referral for an assessment.

Once the couple has sought professional medical advice and investigated the possibility of the presence of Asperger syndrome, they can return to counselling once again.

Seeking specialist help

When a couple knows that one of them has Asperger syndrome, they should request that they receive appropriate specialised counselling for the problems they are facing. This is one of the gains of having sought and received a diagnosis. Both partners will feel understood and that their concerns are being heard if they see a counsellor who specialises in this area and who is familiar with the effects the syndrome may have on the couple's relationship.

The importance of having counsellors specially trained to help people in this situation is slowly being recognised. More and more counsellors and therapists are coming to realise the importance of being able to offer appropriate and beneficial support to couples affected by Asperger syndrome. Training workshops are now available and articles have been written. I cannot express the importance of a counsellor being able to recognise the *possibility* of an individual being affected by Asperger syndrome and to have the confidence to approach the topic with a client. Many couples have described to me their disappointment that they were not aware of Asperger syndrome despite the very obvious signs during their counselling sessions. Ignorance is certainly not bliss in the case of a diagnosis of Asperger syndrome.

PART II

The aim in the second part of this book is to look at some of the problems that living with a partner who has Asperger syndrome (Autism Spectrum Disorder) can present. In what follows are various strategies and ways of coping with difficulties that have worked for others. Most apply equally to women and men who have a partner with Asperger syndrome, regardless of their sexuality. It is, though, impossible to generalise, as what works for one couple will not necessarily work for another – each individual and relationship is unique.

11

LIVING AND COPING WITH ASPERGER SYNDROME (AUTISM SPECTRUM DISORDER)

Each of us is unique

Every human being is unique, just as every couple's relationship is unique. That said, when one partner has Asperger syndrome, all couples for whom this is the case have something in common with each other.

Having the syndrome results in a similar set of problems being created within any intimate relationship. How severe these problems are and how they affect each couple will be dependent on an accumulation of factors. One of these is how well you are able to cope and find better ways in which to deal with problems as they arise. Another important factor is how severely your partner is affected by the syndrome, and in what areas they are particularly affected.

The fact that your partner has formed a long-term intimate relationship with you is a very positive thing as it is likely to mean that they are at the higher, more able end of the spectrum. Many adults with Asperger syndrome never form such relationships. For some this is because they are not interested in developing them; for others the desire is there, but they have neither the social skills nor ability to do so. And for some adults with Asperger syndrome, there can be little motivation to change. They may therefore remain quite rigid within their particular lifestyles or ways, so their relationships do not develop and are prone to fading out very quickly.

Not everyone with Asperger syndrome is the same

Once again, because every person is unique, having Asperger syndrome affects each person in a very individual way. There will be problems with communication, socialising and empathetic thought, but how these manifest varies from person to person. Having Asperger syndrome does not change someone's personality.

It may be that their lives are not full of obsessive interests or rigid routines because not all higher-functioning adults with Asperger syndrome have obvious obsessive tendencies. You may not find major problems around socialising in your relationship, but trying to get your views across could prove impossible.

Your partner may not want to talk about feelings and emotions, but that does not mean they do not have any. Many varied factors play their part in how each person is affected, such as their age, upbringing, capacity for learning and, most importantly, the person they have chosen to share their life with.

A social guide

If you are in an intimate relationship with someone who has Asperger syndrome, you are one of the most important people in their lives. How you approach and cope with problems can make a difference to how they cope with many of the difficulties that having Asperger syndrome can present them with. This is not to say that you will have to take responsibility for everything your partner does, but it is important that you are aware that there are some things that you will be naturally better at.

You will have a strong advantage over your partner in the area of social skills, interaction and communication, and this may be even more the case if your partner is male. In many ways, a person with Asperger syndrome is socially myopic and will rely on you to be their guide in a society that must at times be very confusing.

It is a good idea to know what problems are likely to occur as a direct result of your partner having Asperger syndrome, and what it is they can actually make choices about. One area that my research has pinpointed as being particularly problematic is that of communication between partners and other family members, so this is the subject of the next chapter.

12

IMPROVING COMMUNICATION

Difficulties with communication

Communication or lack of communication seems to be the one area that many men and women cite as being the most problematic in their relationship. This is not surprising considering that difficulties with both verbal and non-verbal forms of communication are strongly indicative, together with other criteria, of Asperger syndrome (Autism Spectrum Disorder).

Communication problems arising when living with a partner who has Asperger syndrome can drive some adults into a state of despair and desperation. People have described this as feeling like they and their partner 'come from different cultures' or are 'talking in different languages'. Trying to find some way of getting a particular point across to partners can lead to frustration, anger and utter despair.

Reasons for these misunderstandings vary from couple to couple. Maybe your partner has a problem with distinguishing the literal from sarcasm, a joke, figure of speech or whatever, and so will interpret most of what is being said in the literal sense of the words. Maybe they find instructions hard to understand and you find yourself repeating the same things over and over again. It could be that they simply do not get the point of what is being said. Something that may appear quite obvious to you will not necessarily be obvious to your partner, and some very awkward and infuriating misunderstandings can develop between you because of this.

Maybe your partner reacts very quickly with anger to something that appears quite trivial, leaving you feeling rejected and dismissed. Perhaps they appear to have a very selective memory, only seeming to remember part of what has been said and then taking it completely out of context. Maybe they just interpret everything that has been said as criticism when, most of the time, all that is being offered is some practical advice.

Whatever form these crossed wires take, it is almost guaranteed that there will be problems with verbal and non-verbal communication between partners in a couple when one has Asperger syndrome.

Good communication is vital

Good quality communication between both partners is very important. Too many misunderstandings in a relationship can cause it to begin to break down. As well as misunderstandings, if there is an almost total absence of communication, this can be very destructive. Indeed, not being heard or acknowledged can be as distressing as being verbally abused.

How something is said and the body language that accompanies it is just as important as what is being said if each partner is to understand what the other is saying. Eye contact, body language and facial expression can help smooth out two-way interactions, and if they do not run smoothly, confusion is inevitable.

Many people with Asperger syndrome, whether male or female, show an impairment in non-verbal communication skills and often have difficulties with the 'pragmatics of speech'. Non-verbal communication refers to the non-verbal signals we give while talking, such as facial expressions and body language, that expand on and clarify what we are saying in words. The way we position our body, our posture and gestures can be valuable indicators as to how we feel and the message we are conveying to another person. We also emphasise particular words and change our tone of voice to convey the meaning of what is being said.

A person with Asperger syndrome will have difficulty with both reading non-verbal and pragmatic signs and sending them. For instance, someone who can look a person in the eye and talk with confidence is likely to be perceived as honest. If your partner does not get these important signals right, you may think they are being evasive or untruthful.

Ambiguity and Asperger syndrome do not mix

If these two ingredients are put together, it can result in instant disaster. It is very important to be precise, direct and straight to the point if your partner has Asperger syndrome. This is because your partner will not always understand double meanings, nor automatically know what had *not* been meant. One woman told her husband that if he did not change he would have to leave and, much to her horror, the next day he left. He took it that that was what she really meant and wanted and, as he did not feel he could change, he left. He could not see that, at the time, she was upset and was desperately trying to get a response out of him that would prompt him to change some of his ways, and that she did not really want him to go.

Ordinarily, this would not happen as someone would know that most people say things when they are upset or angry that they do not necessarily mean. Unfortunately, someone with Asperger syndrome may find underlying meanings very difficult to understand, so it is important that you remember to say what you mean and mean what you say – this alone can prevent many misunderstandings. Sometimes, though, it can make conversing very tiring and lengthy, especially when you are feeling fed up and just wish that your partner would understand the point of what is being said. At such times, take a break and come back to the topic later on. Whatever course you take, however, it is certainly worthwhile remaining clear and precise, as this will make life far easier in the long run.

It is not a case of being awkward

Before knowing about Asperger syndrome, many people may suspect their partners of just being awkward or not trying or wanting to interact and communicate effectively. Once a positive diagnosis has been received, you then know that your partner is not being deliberately evasive or uncommunicative. It is not because they do not *want* to understand what is being said; it is much more likely that they simply do not understand it.

As we have seen, having the syndrome can mean that communication is very difficult if what is being said is not framed in a clear and precise way. This does not mean that your partner is not intelligent and does not have the ability to learn – indeed, it is likely that they will have a higher than average IQ.

If they are given the correct help, support and guidance and have the motivation to learn, they can develop strategies to help them cope and respond more appropriately in communication and social situations. For example, one man agreed with his Asperger wife that when she had to attend work-related social events without him, he would call her on her mobile after about two hours. He agreed to say he had locked himself out of the house (or some other excuse) and to ask if she could come home. This gave her the excuse to leave without appearing rude. His wife struggled with social events and found it difficult to excuse herself if she began to feel overloaded and anxious. Both in the relationship gained by this simple strategy – his wife had an exit strategy for social events and he found she returned home far less stressed.

Your partner is not stupid!

The only type of intelligence affected by Asperger syndrome is social intelligence.

It is likely that your partner has been made to feel stupid many times in his life. As a child, they are likely to have been singled out, identified as 'different' and bullied at school. The bullying was probably quite severe and so, as an adult, they may be very sensitive to any form of perceived ridicule or put-down, especially from you. This could instantly anger them and they may react to the situation as if they were suddenly back in the playground, placing you on the outside, as an enemy.

Once this happens, there is very little chance that you will be able to reach reconciliation quickly. Even when you do, they may not let go and forget what you said. Those with Asperger syndrome can have an excellent memory for dialogue, and their memory of what you said can sometimes seem unfairly selective. It is possible that, in particular, they will remember the negative things to the exclusion of anything else, and perceive them to be a personal verbal attack.

Disclosure

Children with Asperger syndrome sometimes have difficulty revealing what is bothering them. They may have tremendous problems at school and many have a history of severe bullying. This is rarely revealed to their parents or teachers, but is often bottled up inside. These feelings may then be projected on to something else, and it is often the parents who get the worst part of the deal. These children know that home is a safer place to express themselves than anywhere else, and so save up a whole day's worth of anxiety and let it out in a fit of anger when they get home.

In a similar way, this can apply to adults and can be observed when they are meeting with a professional person, where they can be incredibly well mannered and polite throughout the duration of the meeting. In most circumstances, this is not a problem, but when the person is a doctor, psychologist or a counsellor, for instance, this can be quite misleading as this is not how they are usually.

One couple went for couples counselling because the husband, who has Asperger syndrome, refused to communicate with his wife and would become angry if she approached him about it. The couple did not realise at the time that Asperger syndrome was the problem. He behaved impeccably in the counselling room and his wife became very frustrated and angry.

She felt as if she had been labelled as 'the baddie' by both her husband and the counsellor, as though the counsellor thought she was exaggerating the problems. It was a very bad experience for her and the couple did not return to counselling.

How to make the right approach

If there is a particular issue or problem that needs to be sorted out, it will probably be up to you, the non-Asperger partner, to choose the right time and place to discuss it with your partner. A time when you will not be interrupted and there will be no distractions is best, and the atmosphere between you should be as calm and stress-free as possible. If you think about the problem carefully and attempt to remain as objective as possible, and do not use any exaggerations, it is more likely that a solution will be found. If the attempt fails it may be because your partner is not in the right frame of mind or perhaps the timing is wrong. Often, though, it can be the choice of words and the way in which things are said that cause a breakdown in communication.

Here are a few strategies you could try that will I hope make communication run more smoothly.

Give complete messages

Giving complete messages is vital if you want your partner to fully understand what it is you are trying to tell them. Complete messages should contain at least four forms of disclosure: stating the facts, your thoughts, your feelings and what it is you need.

The facts should be based on something you have seen, heard, read or personally experienced. Your interpretation of the facts, though, is likely to be influenced by your own beliefs and opinions, but it is important to be honest about how you feel. Feelings can trigger some strong defensive reactions in both ourselves and others, sometimes leading to anger. Such anger is often used as a defence, especially when feeling sad and vulnerable and self-esteem is running a bit low. It can be employed to disguise vulnerability.

The final stage in giving a complete message is to tell your partner exactly what you need. Although expressing feelings such as insecurity would immediately signal that maybe a hug is needed, this will not always happen when the communication is with a partner who has Asperger syndrome. They will not be able to guess what you want: you have to tell them.

Use complete messages

Using complete messages can take time and practice and it is a skill both you and your partner can learn. One couple I came into contact with had endless arguments about what appeared, on the surface, to be relatively trivial subjects. He described her as always angry and ready to 'attack' him; she was at her wits end and felt frustrated by the constant cycle they seemed to get caught up in. We discussed talking in complete messages and began to practise this skill and put it into operation.

One thing that they often fell out about was the way he would forget to give her a hug when he went to work. The tension would build up throughout breakfast. She would glare at him across the table; he had no idea what he had done wrong but knew she was mad at him. This often resulted in him rushing out of the house as quickly as possible without so much as a goodbye, which left her feeling very rejected and vulnerable. Neither had discussed this pattern or ever said how it made them feel. We worked at putting this into a complete message and this resulted in the couple communicating as follows:

> He: 'I can see by your face that you are mad at me, I think you are about to start shouting at me, I feel afraid because I do not know how to prevent it, I need to get away as quickly as possible.'

She: 'You keep forgetting to give me a hug before you go to work – I think you do it on purpose. It makes me feel very rejected and hurt. I need you to remember to hug me.'

By being able to communicate in complete messages both understood what the other wanted to say and they agreed to put a notice on the door to remind him to give her a hug. When the hug became a habit the notice was no longer needed. She had learned not to disguise her feelings with anger and he had learned that if he gave her a hug, she would be happy and he could enjoy his breakfast.

Always use the word 'I'

It is also important when you are explaining something to your partner, especially your feelings, always to remain in 'adult mode' – that is, always make use of the word 'I', not the word 'you', which can appear to be an accusation. Imagine being on the receiving end of the following – how would you feel?

- 'You have really upset me.'

- 'How could you be so thoughtless?'

- 'Jack's my best mate, you acted like a total bitch to him!'

- 'You really were so selfish tonight.'

- 'Why did you have to be so rude to my mother?'

- 'You think more about your precious (CD collection/ magazines, handbags, etc.) than you do about me.'

All these statements may seem quite justified at the time that they are said, but your partner would interpret them as being critical and 'attacking' them. All sound far better if you rephrase them using the word 'I':

- 'I feel quite upset by what was said earlier – maybe we could try to sort it out.'

- 'I felt that my feelings were not considered earlier on and this has left me feeling not cared for.'

- 'I felt something was bothering you about Jack. He is important to me and so are you. Can we talk about this?'

- 'I felt my needs weren't acknowledged tonight and that has upset me.'

- 'Did my mother say something to upset you? I could not understand why you said ... to her.'

- 'I would like you to spend more time with me, I feel lonely sometimes.'

When partners interact, it is important that each takes responsibility for their own feelings and does not make assumptions about what the other is feeling. This is important to remember as it will give you a far better chance of getting your partner to listen and not interpret what is being said as a critical attack on them, which could just make them withdraw or become defensive.

How to respond and not react

An important lesson to learn when developing communication skills is to respond, but not react. This can make the difference between a conversation running smoothly and reaching a satisfactory conclusion or rapidly escalating into a heated debate.

It is not always easy when you are feeling tired or frustrated to stop yourself from reacting to a situation or a statement made by your partner. However, the results of doing so are nearly always negative and achieve little, whereas responding, maybe with a question and giving your partner time and the feeling that it is safe to reply, achieves a far more positive outcome. To react can often sound like you are blaming your partner for something, but to respond is to remain open and not accusatory.

For example, one non-Asperger man who was in a relationship was accused by his male partner of thinking more of his friends than he did of him. His immediate reaction was one of defence and attack:

> 'How dare you criticise me about caring for my friends, I do everything for you and you can't even be bothered to notice. You don't appreciate anything about me, at least my friends take the time to talk to me!'

The consequence was an instant row.

Responding instead of reacting might first require a couple of deep breaths to help remain calm. This also gives a little time to think of an appropriate response. An appropriate response should be presented in the form of a question or using a complete message, and the reaction above could be replaced with:

> 'You say I think more of my friends than you. I think I give a lot to our relationship and this is unjustified. I feel very hurt and need you to explain what exactly it is that has made you feel like this.'

The Asperger partner will now be aware of the effect their accusation has had on their partner and have the opportunity to be more precise and explain. In this case, it turned out that the Asperger partner was feeling insecure as he felt his partner always seemed happier with his friends than he did with him, and this gave them the opportunity to plan and arrange more quality time together.

Never assume

You should never assume that you know what your partner is thinking or that they know what you are thinking. This can be especially problematic if you are a woman living with a partner who has Asperger syndrome.

Most women can be very intuitive and pick up on an atmosphere and someone else's inner feelings quite quickly.

They are often far better at using and reading non-verbal language than most men. This strong intuition gives women an advantage over men at interpreting non-verbal communication and, in most circumstances, this can work to a woman's benefit – unless, that is, she is living with a partner who has Asperger syndrome. Then, the non-verbal signals and body language sent out by her partner will not always accurately reflect what he is actually thinking or feeling. This is evident from the poor eye contact that can be part of the non-verbal behaviour of people with Asperger syndrome, male or female. Evasive eye contact may give the impression that a person is lying. Often, though, in the case of people with Asperger syndrome, they are not lying, they are just poor communicators. It may also be that they smile or laugh at the wrong time and their partners are left thinking that they are making fun of them or not taking them seriously, when it is more likely that they do not know how to react. A smile may make someone happy, but, at the wrong time, it can appear very patronising. Many of the non-verbal reactions that adults with Asperger syndrome use have been learned; they are not always automatic, and so have to be thought through.

Never presume that your partner automatically knows or has picked up on what you are feeling. To expect a person with Asperger syndrome to know what someone is thinking, no matter how intimate they are, would be like expecting a blind person to guess what someone is holding in their hand without giving them any clues. Your partner cannot read minds and does not know instinctively from your expressions or body language what it is they are expected to do or say.

One way that your partner can be helped to understand what is expected of them is to use a written form of communication, such as letter writing, and this is described in the next chapter.

13

GETTING THE MESSAGE ACROSS

Writing things down

Tony Attwood strongly recommends that it is simpler for each partner to write things down in letter or note form than to try and express verbally what each is trying to say or ask (Attwood 1998). This idea has certainly proved successful in my own experience of counselling couples when one of the partners has Asperger syndrome (Autism Spectrum Disorder), as it can offer great insight into what is really going on for both partners. One man with Asperger syndrome whom I interviewed for the first edition of this book was only able to communicate his deeper feelings through letter writing, and he did this with profound literal accuracy and a great depth of feeling. The letters proved invaluable to his wife and compensated for what he never said. Letter writing gave him the time to think about what he wanted to say or what was bothering him.

For some couples writing things down, such as lists or reminders, works very well and can make giving instructions or directions for something far less complicated. One man bought his Asperger wife a journal so she could write down her feelings when she felt overwhelmed and struggled to communicate with him. Over time she shared parts of her journal with him and this gave him an insight into how she felt and how he could make improvements in his responses to her and develop strategies to help her cope. Equally relevant was the woman who brought her Asperger partner a diary which he used to write down important appointments, any arrangements he made with her and the children, or any jobs he had agreed to do on a particular day. It proved to be an absolute life-saver once it became part of his daily routine to look in it.

Getting a response can be a problem when using letter writing, however, as an issue may require an answer or a response quite quickly. It may be that your partner will just read the note and that's it! The note goes into their pocket and then they just forget all about it. If nothing is mentioned, you may become impatient and so demand an answer, which could produce a defensive reaction rather than an understanding response, and suddenly the relationship is back to square one, leaving you feeling unheard and misunderstood. You could arrange between you beforehand that if a letter is given, then an answer, or at least an acknowledgement, should be given within 24 hours, either in letter form or verbally.

Incentive, motivation and change

One of the reasons that your partner may ignore what you are saying to them or asking them to do is because they have not been given any valid reason to do otherwise. Writing letter after letter, list after list and pinning them up on noticeboards all over the house will make no difference at all unless they have an incentive to respond or do what you have asked of them. An incentive will increase their motivation, which will produce a change.

If your partner knows that if they do a certain thing it will make you happy and that, in return, you will, for example, go with them to the botanic gardens or give them some time out to pursue their favourite interest, there will be some incentive to respond. Sometimes, if they know that doing something means that you will not get upset and their life will be easier, this alone can be enough of an incentive. If they understand what it is they need to do, knowing that in return for their endeavours they will get something in return, they will be motivated. However, the payback for their actions has to be something that directly benefits them – not you, not the children, not the dog, just them.

One couple found an ideal compromise. The male Asperger partner loved old cars and was quite an expert at restoring them.

He would do this whenever he had any spare time, but at the expense of doing anything else. His partner, on the other hand, enjoyed the theatre, but he would not go with her, as he was always too occupied working on his cars, so they struck up a deal. Every other week she would spend a few hours with him, either helping him polish up the upholstery in one of his cars, or visiting a motor show, and every other week he would go to the theatre with her. This worked well and enabled them to share something together.

Making use of the telephone and internet

Letter writing may help people say what is on their mind although it is likely that email or social media can be used to an even better effect than letter writing, as many people with Asperger syndrome enjoy spending time on the computer and the internet.

Partners with Asperger syndrome have also said that they find it easier to communicate on the telephone as they feel both safer and less confused in this situation. It does not require them to use any facial expressions or eye contact, which can make them feel uneasy. Neither do they have to try to read others' expressions, so they are able just to concentrate on what is being said.

Talking with the lights turned down

Talking with the lights turned down can also reduce the confusion of mixed messages caused by misunderstanding non-verbal language, and may feel more intimate than writing a letter or sending an email.

Your partner may feel safer and more at ease when they cannot see your face clearly as they might find it confusing to try to understand your facial expressions *and* listen to your words and understand them at the same time. Try to keep your sides of the conversation equal in length and content, and take turns talking.

I normally recommend that couples try this while they are sitting together in the living room. I suggest that they turn off the television, turn down the lights, sit together, hold hands or whatever is most comfortable for them. It is a good idea to take the phone off the hook, make sure the children are in bed or out for the evening and then each take the time to talk and listen. Listening is just as important as talking, and you may have to be very patient and give your partner the time and space they need to say what they want to say. It is important to hear through what your partner is saying without jumping in and making assumptions. If there is any opportunity to encourage them to talk about what is bothering them, it is important to make the most of it to reduce their anxiety and ensure your peace of mind.

Learning to listen

One of the reasons that your partner may not understand what you have said is due to the way they may focus their attention on just a small part of what you are saying and will not appear to have heard the rest. When this happens, repeat what was said and perhaps explain it in a different way. Check they have understood the meaning behind what was said by asking them to repeat it to you in their own words.

One exercise that I found very useful when working with couples is the 'listening task'. Each partner takes turns in talking for two minutes about a completely neutral subject. During this time the other has to listen and not interrupt. Afterwards they repeat what they have heard to the partner who spoke. Each partner takes turns each day to do this. As both become more equipped at listening, the time could be extended or more personal subjects talked about. Experiment with this exercise and see what works for you.

Dealing with one subject at a time

Too much information can cause sensory overload for your partner regardless of whether they are male or female. This is why using a written form of communication or talking on the telephone may produce better results than a face-to-face conversation. Simultaneously interpreting non-verbal communication and understanding what is being said requires a lot of concentration. Also, using these other methods, the amount of information contained in each communication can be decreased, which will improve the chances of it being understood.

It is also important to deal with only one subject at a time. A statement such as the following example may cause utter chaos and produce only a negative reaction:

> 'Well, what are you going to do about fixing the leak in the bathroom? Should we call a plumber? I have been asking you to do something for days – why do you always ignore me? You're just like your father – he never listened to a thing your mother said. I am sick of it. Well don't just stand there, shut the front door, I've just made a pot of tea.'

After such an onslaught, the Asperger partner may run the other way, freeze or react with anger. It is doubtful that they will either fix the tap or want a cup of tea. It is important, therefore, to remember only to ask one question about one subject at a time.

Summing up – the golden rules of communication

Here are the main points to remember when communicating with your partner:

- no ambiguous messages
- no double meanings
- use complete messages

- use the word 'I', not 'you'
- give an incentive
- never presume to know what your partner is thinking or feeling
- be clear, precise and straight to the point
- deal with one subject at a time
- find time and space for your partner to reply and tell you what their perspective on the situation is
- use any medium that helps to improve communication.

14

ANGER

Anger can be an issue

Some men and women living with a partner who has Asperger syndrome (Autism Spectrum Disorder) have reported that their partners have a profound fear of confrontation and will do anything to avoid a display of anger directed at them. Those with the syndrome whom I have interviewed have all said that this is so, and it seems that this is especially the case when it is the male partner who has Asperger syndrome.

This fear manifests itself in the form of being unreasonably defensive, not speaking, leaving the room – anything rather than have their partner direct their anger at them. One woman's Asperger partner would disappear for days when she became angry with him. He reasoned that if he stayed away long enough, eventually she would have to calm down. The trouble was that, by the time he returned, she would be completely frantic after having contacted all the local hospitals, their family and friends, only to find out that he had spent the past couple of days looking at medieval church architecture.

A heightened sensitivity to anger

For men and women with Asperger syndrome, the fear of anger seems to be completely out of proportion. It could be that you find yourself being accused of being angry when you are not. It is often that the partner with Asperger syndrome misreads the signals and thinks a particular look or tone of voice represents anger.

This can be very frustrating when you are trying to discuss a matter with your partner and before you know it, everything is out of proportion and a row is developing. You need to learn to recognise this pattern and stop it before it develops, either by ending the conversation, changing the subject or agreeing to save it until later. In the counselling room I suggest that couples make rules beforehand and agree that they will bring the discussion to a quick end if it becomes too uncomfortable.

One couple used a colour system to let each other know how they felt: green stood for 'okay', amber 'starting to feel unsure', and red meant 'I want to stop this now'. The non-Asperger partner would ask what colour the other felt: if they said red, for instance, then they would leave the subject until things felt calmer.

Anger should not be used as a means of expression or to get your point across. Some men and women reported trying to suppress their anger for this reason. This can have a detrimental effect on both mental and physical health.

Depression can be the result of anger turned inwards

Non-Asperger women more than men reported suffering from depression. Some had probably realised that anger was a useless emotion in their relationship and so tried to suppress it. This suppressed anger may develop into depression, and the long-term effects of this can be deterioration in both the mental and physical health of the person involved.

It is important that ways of releasing anger are explored. Many have tried different therapies, exercise programmes, counselling and outside support to help them vent their anger in a controlled and safe way.

Finding a positive channel for anger

The most effective and appropriate way for the non-Asperger partner to alleviate the effects of suppressed anger will depend on their individual circumstances, age, lifestyle, culture, financial situation and overall level of physical fitness.

For those who are physically able, sports of any kind can be a great outlet, whether it is gentle exercise, such as golf, yoga, Tai Chi, swimming or walking, or more physically demanding sports, such as squash, football, running or aerobics. All of these can help to release stored-up aggression and energy in a positive way. One woman related how she had joined the local running club and ended up completing the London Marathon!

Other men and women I contacted relied on their religious faith to help get them through. They found that the support they received from their religious group or through prayer to be of tremendous value.

Some of the adults I spoke with had found individual counselling to be beneficial. It gave them time to talk about anxieties and to express their anger to someone who could offer support and understand how they felt. They found this to be an excellent way of releasing frustrations. When you are seeking counselling it is important that the counsellor selected is aware of, and understands, the effects of Asperger syndrome on a relationship.

Respect

For any relationship to work there needs to be respect between a couple, and no one has the right to be abusive towards the other. In relationships where one person has Asperger syndrome it may sometimes be the case that it is the non-Asperger partner who is being angry and abusive towards their partner with Asperger syndrome. I have found that some individuals with Asperger syndrome show a very high tolerance to abusive behaviour and will tolerate and stay in relationships long after they should have left. The abuse that is tolerated may be physical, verbal, emotional or financial. If you believe you are being abusive towards your partner then seek help and if necessary, anger management.

This way you will not only learn to show respect towards your partner but you will also find respect for yourself.

What about Asperger anger?

Anger can explode quite suddenly and seemingly for no reason in some individuals with Asperger syndrome. I call this the 'fight response'. It may be something quite trivial that triggers their anger, and sometimes this can result in the nearest object to hand being broken. The suddenness and strength of the anger can be quite frightening to witness, especially when it is directed at you or your children – the chances are that it will be completely irrational and unexpected.

It is important to try not to return this with your own anger (easier said than done), as your partner's anger will normally diffuse very quickly. Indeed, they will probably wonder what everyone is so upset about and could appear quite unaware what a painful and disturbing experience it was for you.

Some men and women reported instances of their partner's anger being channelled into road rage or directed at some innocent bystander, and having tried to reason with them about the unfairness and irrationality of it. It can be very difficult to try and discuss your partner's anger with them. At times when they seem to have heard what has been said and change looks hopeful, this may be short-lived. Adults with Asperger syndrome appear to go onto 'automatic pilot' when faced with particular situations and certain triggers are present.

For example, one woman's husband used to get very irate when anyone drove too close behind him, and he would go to extreme and sometimes dangerous lengths to challenge the other driver's presence. He saw the other driver as the enemy and would become so focused on watching the other driver in the mirror that he was in danger of not concentrating on the road ahead and causing an accident. This scared his wife and she had told him how she felt. Her partner, though, seemed unable to break this pattern and to ignore the car behind him. In cases like this it may be a good idea to talk to a professional as the adult with Asperger syndrome is often more likely to listen to a third party than their partner. In this example the couple discussed it in counselling, and the woman's husband agreed that whenever this happened he would pull over when it was safe to do so and let the car behind pass.

Flight is more likely than fight

For the majority of men and women with Asperger syndrome it appears to be more likely that they will react to stress by shutting down, not communicating and keeping their distance from their partner. Some non-Asperger partners struggle with this and make the mistake of seeing it as a rejection. It is rarely a rejection, however; it is rather their partner needing time out and space. Many men and women with Asperger syndrome have a profound fear of confrontation and will take to their heels and run if they feel threatened, regardless of whether the threat is real or perceived. My recommendation to the non-Asperger partner in times such as these is to use the space to do other things and to try to feel secure in the knowledge that their partner will return in their own time. Having said this, for many men and women it is understandably a time that leaves them feeling very lonely.

15

SEX

Loneliness in the bedroom

Some women and men living with a partner who has Asperger syndrome (Autism Spectrum Disorder) reported a complete lack of sexual intimacy in their relationship. In some cases, sexual intercourse had only occurred once or twice and then ceased altogether, leaving the non-Asperger partner feeling very rejected, unloved and wondering what they had done wrong. Both men and women with Asperger syndrome have reported finding sexual intimacy difficult and not thinking of it as a necessary part of the relationship.

It is important to be aware that this is often not a reflection of a lack of love for you, but is more likely part of Asperger syndrome. Those with Asperger syndrome may not always require close physical or sexual contact with another person and would rather masturbate or abstain from sex totally. For some adults living with a partner with Asperger syndrome, the sexual side of the relationship is not very important to them and so they are more able to cope with a lack of it, while others may channel their sexual energy elsewhere.

Those who feel that sexual intimacy is very important to them do not cope with its absence very well, and so this area of the relationship soon becomes one that breeds frustration and bitterness. Unless the Asperger partner is willing to try and sort something out about it and listen to what is being said, the situation will probably not change. Eventually they will have to make their own decisions as to whether or not the plusses in the relationship compensate for the loss of sexual intimacy.

There are more books now being written on the sexual side of Asperger syndrome, and some psycho-sexual therapists are becoming more aware of the implications this has on how they work with Asperger couples. If you feel you and your partner would benefit from such support, it is worth exploring what help might be available.

Sometimes sex can become an obsession

It is not always the case that adults with Asperger syndrome do not have or want sex. For some, the sexual side of the relationship is not unlike that of any other couple, and both parties report a happy and fulfilling sex life together.

In a few cases, however, the partner becomes obsessive in their endeavour to achieve perfection in their sexual role, and practises until they feel they have achieved the most perfect and rewarding sexual routine that they can. Some non-Asperger women reported that they were left feeling very used, as if they were being experimented on.

There is also a danger that once the 'perfect' routine has become established, it will not be changed. Restricted by this routine, sex can then become regimented. Although they may be putting a lot of effort into pleasing their partner, the whole sexual act can come to feel like a process that follows a set order, from beginning to end.

So what happens if you are not satisfied by your sex life and want to try something else? An attempt to do something different or to change the routine could cause confusion and misunderstandings. Your partner may find this need to change very difficult and take it as a criticism of their lovemaking abilities. They may react negatively and you could end up feeling ignored and unheard, the self-esteem and confidence in both of you shattered.

Sex is a form of communication

Communication has been highlighted as problematic in relationships when one partner has Asperger syndrome, and as sex is also a form of communication, it is no exception. Sometimes the reason for sexual problems could be easily rectified if the couple could discuss their differences in clearer detail; more importantly, the adult without Asperger syndrome should not make any assumptions about their partner's behaviour. Things that might seem quite trivial to others may prove to be of great importance to the partner with Asperger syndrome.

For example, one Asperger partner suddenly refused to have any sexual contact with his wife. He became very unresponsive and unaffectionate. This had lasted for over 12 months when eventually the couple came for counselling, which was at the request of the woman in the relationship. Time and patience were given while the partner with Asperger syndrome was allowed to explore his feelings and reasons for not having sex. He talked about his toiletries, and in particular his toothbrush. He had a certain way of leaving his razor, shaving foam and toothbrush in a particular order on the shelf behind the sink every morning. Every evening when he came to brush his teeth, he found his wife had placed his toothbrush in a cup with everyone else's. This annoyed him immensely and by the time he got into bed he was too angry to even touch his wife. After discussing this further, his wife was able to understand how important it was to him and agreed that she would leave the toothbrush where it was. Their love life slowly returned to normal. If the woman in the relationship had not initiated their need for support within the counselling services, the issues might not have been resolved.

When the non-Asperger partner is the male it seems to be less likely that he will suggest or seek out support as he may be reluctant to discuss it with a third party. This is not surprising when we look at the research from the Centers for Disease Control and Prevention (CDCP) which discovered that men are 100 per cent less likely to go to the doctor for preventative care than women (CDCP 2001).

If you feel you are struggling to resolve sexual issues between you and your partner, it may be that you need some support and guidance. Keeping quiet will not help you or your partner work it out, and sometimes the answer might be quite simple when it is shared with a professional in a safe environment.

Where does the information about sex come from?

Just as most adults with Asperger syndrome learn how to socialise and interact from books, television programmes or the internet, this can also be the case for sexual activities. What they say and do in bed may depend on what they have read or seen on television. Men and women have reported their partners coming out with some most unusual statements in the middle of sex, and often being shocked by what can sometimes seem quite crude remarks that are completely out of character.

Others will ask rather strange, clinical questions that may make sex feel like a biological experiment.

These statements or questions often come from something Asperger partners have seen on television or the internet, read in a magazine or overheard at work. It is wise to have an idea where the information comes from as this may affect how they regard their role and their partner's role in a sexual relationship. If they are reading pornographic magazines, visit sites on the internet or are receiving information from an unreliable friend, they may be led to believe that behaviour which their partner finds quite unacceptable is appropriate.

There are plenty of good and reliable reading materials around, and some books offer a visual guide that may make it easier for a partner with Asperger syndrome. If either you or your partner finds it hard to talk about sex, consider going to counselling together or seek the help of a psycho-sexual therapist.

For most relationships, it is important to know that sex is something very special, shared between partners, and not just a performance or simply a means to an end.

Sensory sensitivity

Sensory sensitivity can play a strong role in why sex does not always go well, and may become fraught with anxiety and misunderstandings. Not all, but many, men and women with Asperger syndrome have a heightened sensitivity to their environment and the noises, smells, sights, textures and tastes that surround them. Be aware what these areas are, otherwise misunderstandings are bound to occur.

For example, a man described how his female partner had refused to have any physical contact with him, and this progressed to the point that they slept in separate rooms and sex was never on the agenda. The couple discovered that she was affected by Asperger syndrome, and as a consequence sought professional help to work at their relationship. The man described how lonely and rejected he felt by his partner and how he could not understand why she was so repulsed by him whenever he tried to get close to her. The counsellor explored the idea of sensory sensitivity and it was revealed that the female partner had a highly sensitive reaction to certain smells. One of those smells was garlic. Further exploration discovered that two years earlier her partner had been diagnosed with a hyperactive thyroid, and a dietician had recommended including garlic in his diet. He followed this advice and over time developed quite a taste for it. Consequently the smell of his body odour and breath was tainted with garlic. His partner was repulsed by this and had since refused any physical approach from him. Her fear of confrontation had prevented her from saying what the problem was, especially as no one else seemed bothered by it. The solution was simple as the man was more than happy to omit garlic from his diet if it meant getting his partner's affection back, and before too long they were sharing both a bed and a physical relationship together.

Check out if your partner is affected by sensory sensitivity and remember that this can manifest itself in many ways, from the distraction of a ticking clock in the bedroom to the feel and texture of certain nightwear.

Getting it right from the start

If your relationship is quite a new one, then it is crucial that both of you start as you mean to go on. It is helpful if you can be patient with your partner and try to tell them in a precise and clear way what you want in bed and what you are prepared to do. If your relationship is well established, it may be harder to change things, but not impossible.

It is important when communicating about sex not to be ambiguous and not to give double messages. Your partner cannot read your mind – they do not know what you want or do not want unless you tell them. Whether or not your relationship is a new one, stress to your partner that you will not want the same things every time, that your needs will change. Reassure them that you will tell them if there is something you do not want, so they will know if they are doing something wrong.

If you are a non-Asperger woman in a heterosexual relationship, perhaps explain a woman's menstrual cycle, pointing out that at certain times of the month you may be more responsive than others. Be sure your partner knows your different reactions to him are not because of something he has done wrong, but that this is just the way most women are and that needs and sexual appetites change.

It is important that both of you feel comfortable about what you are doing. No one in a sexual relationship should have to do anything they feel uncomfortable with. As your partner may have more difficulty with discussing sexual issues, check that they are happy with the lovemaking and what is being shared together.

Be positive

When you discuss sex with your partner, do so in a sensitive way, taking care not to sound critical. Positive and constructive examples should be given of how sex can be enjoyed more together, so that your partner knows exactly what you want. If possible, explain these in a visual way. Try to find a time when you will not be disturbed and the atmosphere is calm and relaxed. Choose your words carefully and be tactful, suggesting rather than demanding, and respect each other's freedom of choice. Follow the golden rules for communication discussed earlier.

Infidelity

In most cases, men and women reported that they had complete trust in their partner's fidelity, and for many this was a very positive aspect of their relationship. In Debbie Then's book, she reported that 50 per cent of men in the general population are likely to 'stray' (Then 1997), yet 80 per cent of the non-Asperger women I contacted in my original research were totally convinced that their husbands were faithful and would remain that way. The security this creates is a huge plus in any relationship and may mean that women tolerate the more negative effects of Asperger syndrome in their relationships.

I have found over the years that it is just as unlikely for an Asperger woman to be unfaithful if she is truly committed to the relationship, and this is equally seen as a bonus to their partners. It needs to be said, however, that for those rare men and women with Asperger syndrome who are unfaithful, this can become a pattern that is very hard to change, and it is likely that they will justify the infidelity. If there is no remorse then it is unlikely that their partner will be able to forgive or learn to trust them again.

16

PARENTING

When the parent with Asperger syndrome (Autism Spectrum Disorder) is female

In her interview with Professor Tony Attwood, Liane Holliday Willey discussed her difficulties understanding her non-Asperger children. Holliday Willey described the lengths she went to rectify this, and still openly admits she sometimes got it wrong. She stated how well adjusted her children were and attributed this to the fact she cared (Holliday Willey and Attwood 1998). Being a parent with Asperger syndrome presents with a set of difficulties, but it does not make a person a bad parent – that is down to personality alone. Holliday Willey's book, *Pretending To Be Normal* (1999), gives a wonderful insight into being a wife and a mother with Asperger syndrome. It is important that female Asperger partners are supported and the childcare shared so that they are able to take time out and look after themselves and their own needs. Do not automatically presume that as a woman she will just know what to do or how to deal with the children, as her capacity to mind read will be limited.

Pregnancy for the non-Asperger woman

Pregnancy, childbirth and parenting can be especially problematic in a relationship if you are the non-Asperger partner with an Asperger man. This section is written specifically for you.

Pregnancy is a time when bonding is very important, but for some women I spoke to it was quite a lonely time, as their partner was very reluctant to have any sexual contact with them, leaving them feeling unwanted and undesirable. For some men with Asperger syndrome this may be because they fear that they will do some harm to their unborn child, and so they feel they should not maintain sexual intimacy during this time. This fear may come from mixed messages about pregnancy received in childhood and adolescence.

Partners should be involved as much as possible with the pregnancy, with a clear explanation of exactly what is happening physically, using visual means if possible. They should be encouraged to ask questions and made to feel very much a part of the whole pregnancy.

Giving birth

It has been reported that some Asperger fathers-to-be did not want to be present at the birth of their child. One woman relayed how her partner quite simply did not turn up at the hospital, which caused her to feel very alone at a time that should have been one of sharing.

Unpredictable and stressful social situations can be quite traumatic for someone with Asperger syndrome, and one of the reasons the birth of their child may be avoided is because they may not have any idea what their role will be and what will be expected of them. If possible, watch a video on childbirth together so that your Asperger partner knows exactly what it will be like and what you want them to do.

It is very difficult at a time like this for non-Asperger mothers-to-be to have to worry about their partner – they will probably feel that their partner should be worrying about them rather than the other way round. This can leave some women feeling cheated out of what should be a loving, caring, shared experience.

If possible (usually it is positively encouraged), both should arrange to go along together to antenatal classes and visit the labour and maternity wards at the hospital where they are planning to have the baby to meet one or more of the midwives or hospital staff. This will help make the forthcoming birthplace feel more familiar and less threatening. Asperger partners should be encouraged to ask questions to help them understand what a very necessary and important part of the whole birth experience they are.

Life after birth

Looking after a baby seems, in most cases where the father has Asperger syndrome, to have been left entirely up to the mother as the father takes on the role of a distant observer. Some women have not found this to be a problem if, as with the financial side of the relationship, they prefer to be in control of the situation and the main decision maker. Other women, however, found this a desperately lonely time and felt at times that they were surviving on the same level as a one-parent family, with little or no practical or emotional support from their partner.

This scenario can be played out in any relationship. Not all men, whether they have Asperger syndrome or not, want to participate in looking after a baby. They may find this stage of child development especially difficult, and for some it can even be quite frightening. What is probably different about the situation when the father has Asperger syndrome is that they may display a lack of empathy towards their partner and do not appear to appreciate how much hard work, emotionally and physically, looking after a new baby can be. If you have an understanding doctor, or know of another professional who understands Asperger syndrome, ask if they could talk to your partner. Your partner may be able to tell the doctor or professional what is bothering them and how they feel about the baby, and the doctor or professional may be able to offer them some advice or extra information. Try all avenues open to you, and if your partner is still unable to offer you any consideration or appreciation, then you may find that you have to find this emotional support elsewhere.

Negotiate the rules

As the children grow, Asperger partners, whether male or female, may have problems both in making themselves understood and in being understood by the children. It is common in people with Asperger syndrome not to discriminate between ages, and it could be particularly difficult for an Asperger partner to talk to the children as children and to be aware of what levels of development and maturity they have reached. Their expectations of their children's capabilities may be set a lot higher than they are actually capable of achieving, and this can cause confusion for all concerned.

Some may not know or understand what they are expected to do or say to the children. For example, one non-Asperger woman described how her nine-year-old son had brought home his report for his parents to read. His father read through the report quite quickly and then, without a word to his son about how well he had done, wrote a lengthy reply to the headmaster. He complained that he was unable to read the English teacher's comments and asked how she could possibly teach his son when her handwriting was illegible. What he had not done in all this was to tell his son what an excellent school report he had brought home; he was only able to focus on the English teacher's handwriting. His wife tried to explain to him that he was missing the point, but it was not until he had written and sent in his letter that he could tell his son it was a good report.

You will often need to state the obvious and always give very clear and precise messages, so that your partner understands what they are supposed to do or say. It is very important that you negotiate the rules between yourselves and both try to stick to them.

If you have a problem trying to negotiate rules and boundaries, and if there is a problem enforcing these rules, then you could try talking it over with a third party, such as a school counsellor or teacher. Making use of noticeboards, lists or diaries is also useful. One woman had lists all over the house, even in the bathroom, giving clear instructions on hanging up the towels, putting the seat down on the toilet (so the youngest did not fall down into the bowl) and flushing the toilet. Experiment with whatever methods work best in your household. If it turns out to be a useful and helpful strategy, then it should be put into practice on a daily basis. Children need a consistent, loving and caring upbringing, and it is you, the non-Asperger partner, who might find yourself being left with most of the responsibility for seeing that they are provided with this.

Teenage terrors – the Asperger nightmare

Parenting may have been fairly straightforward while the children were young enough to obey commands and rules without arguing about them, but all this can change when they hit adolescence, start bringing friends home and answering back.

Your Asperger partner probably never understood their own adolescence, so it is very unlikely that they will understand it in their own children. They may find their disruptive routines, changeable timetables, faddy eating habits, unpredictable moods, answering back and constant demand for lifts an Asperger nightmare. It could feel like there is an additional teenager in the house and you may wonder who is the harder work – the children or your partner.

One woman's husband used to spend his time trying to get his daughter to be tidier. He went as far as putting his daughter's homework in the rubbish bin because she had left it on the kitchen table. He felt this was quite justified and would not apologise for his actions. The whole family was in an uproar and it was his wife who had to write a letter to the school to try to smooth things over. As the non-Asperger partner, you will have to be the mediator, negotiator, referee, rule-maker, wiper up of tears, confidante – in other words, all things to all people.

If your children know about Asperger syndrome, you could ask them to be more sensitive and to try to understand why there are some things that their father/mother does not get right or understand. It should be explained to them that things that cause their father/mother stress and frustration should be avoided. House rules need to be negotiated for the whole family.

You will need all the help you can get. As you will be the one giving out all the emotional energy, you should be aware of your own needs at this time – otherwise, you will be left feeling completely drained and very alone. Try to make some time for yourself and put your needs first at times, whether this takes the form of a night out with friends or a hobby or sport that gets you out of the house. It is vital that you have time and space that is completely separate from your partner and the children, where you can just unwind and be yourself, free from any demands.

17

MONEY MATTERS

Sorting out the finances

In most cases, the couples I contacted reported that it was the non-Asperger partner who looked after the financial side of things in the relationship and largely, this seemed to work quite well. Problems could arise, however, if the Asperger partner had an expensive special interest, such as collecting rare old coins or buying goods online. Be aware of what is happening to the finances, especially if money is not abundant. In a few cases where the non-Asperger partner was not allowed any control of the finances at all, there were massive debts.

Whether or not poor money management skills are a consequence of Asperger syndrome (Autism Spectrum Disorder) is impossible to say as I have also talked to men and women who say their Asperger partners are excellent at dealing with the finances. Adults with Asperger syndrome often show an inclination towards extremes, by either being very capable at doing a particular task or by finding it very difficult. This area has not been studied sufficiently, however, and certainly, financial problems may occur in any relationship, whether one of the partners has Asperger syndrome or not. The difference Asperger syndrome makes in a relationship is that it introduces an extra level of difficulty when trying to discuss financial problems. It may be hard to get your Asperger partner to talk about monetary matters and to establish the rules and boundaries.

Knowing what is being spent

It is important to know what is happening on the financial front regardless of whether you are male or female. If at all possible, either deal with the finances yourself or at least maintain some form of independence. This is not so difficult to do today as it was a few decades ago, as many women now are able to control their own finances. As mentioned earlier, telling others is not high on the list of priorities for people with Asperger syndrome, so it could be the case that you will be the last to know about any financial problems that have been building up. This is probably because your partner is frightened of telling you what is happening and the reaction it might provoke, which is especially likely to be the case when the money is being spent on their special interest.

18

SPECIAL INTERESTS

It can be a bonus

Most of the adults I contacted said that their Asperger partners had a special interest, and most said they did not find it particularly problematic in the relationship when compared to other areas, such as communication. In fact, some said that their partner's special interest was a bonus! Many were happy that their partner had something to interest them and keep them busy. One woman remarked that at least he was not chasing other women or 'living in the pub'.

Such special interests are likely to be solitary pursuits, for example, collecting certain objects, exploring old churches or running. Life with someone who has Asperger syndrome (Autism Spectrum Disorder) may involve feeling similar to a 'golf widow' or a widower. The special interest may also be linked to the person's field of work, perhaps in engineering or computers. Simon Baron-Cohen found that, statistically, engineering occupations featured more predominantly in families in which Asperger syndrome was present (Baron-Cohen *et al.* 1997).

Some of the special interests reported were a little unusual, even quite bizarre. One woman said that her husband bought copies of every hi-fi magazine he could lay his hands on, and had been doing so for most of his life. The problem was that he would not throw any of them away, and the collection had become so large that she was unable to get into their spare room, as it was literally full from floor to ceiling with magazines. Eventually there was no longer any room for anything else in their home, so they were looking for a bigger house.

For most couples, the partner's special interest is not an issue and becomes a way of life. As long as it does not push the family into debt, it should be tolerated and can be a very good talking point.

If obsessions do become a problem financially, it is important that this is dealt with in its earliest stages and not allowed to escalate. If it is possible for the non-Asperger partner to take charge of the finances, then this is often the best solution. Those who have managed to do this have found it a tremendous relief as then neither partner has to worry about what is happening with the money.

When a special interest is unacceptable

Although it appears to be quite rare in cases of Asperger syndrome, sometimes the partner's special interest is something that the other partner feels is totally unacceptable. It may be something that is counter to what would normally be permissible within a close relationship, and then both partners need to do something about it. For instance, if the Asperger partner is obsessed with sex, pornography (possibly spending time seeking it on the internet) or other women or men in a sexual way and has extramarital affairs, the other partner has the same rights as anyone else in a relationship when boundaries are being crossed. If they find pornography offensive or are concerned that a certain special interest is not setting a good example for the children, then they have the right to act and either end the relationship or demand that things change.

If your partner will not change and is also aware that their behaviour is unacceptable to you, then you have to make a choice: do you or don't you want the relationship to continue?

Another example comes from a non-Asperger man who described his partner's attachment to animals and how she discovered that some pet stores reduced their stock by putting animals down if they were not housed before a specific age. This applied mainly to rodents. His wife then went on a mission to save them all, and if she could not find them homes, took them into their own home. Before long the house was overrun with animals and cages – she took great care of them and he tolerated this for many months. However, when they found their way into their bedroom, due to lack of space, he took action and refused to allow any more into their home. In this case it caused the breakdown of their relationship – hence the importance of starting as you mean to go on. If your partner seems to be developing an interest that could be detrimental to your relationship together, put down the rules and reach a compromise before it becomes an issue.

Sharing interests

Some couples I spoke to shared similar interests; many reported that they enjoyed going to the theatre together, listening to music or seeing films at the cinema, for example. Many couples I have encountered shared the same religious beliefs and their faith was very important to them. As long as you are prepared to do things your partner's way and are able to relate to an area of interest, then this can be an excellent way for you to feel closer to each other and to share things together. Also, if the interest is something new to you, there is the bonus that you will become an expert on something that you previously knew little or nothing about.

ROUTINES

Never-ending routines

Some adults with Asperger syndrome (Autism Spectrum Disorder) have some very rigid routines that they feel very strongly have to be followed through in the same order every time. It may be, for example, the 'getting ready for work' routine, the 'daily cleansing' routine, the 'cleaning the house' routine or the 'eating at the table' routine. Once a routine becomes established, it can soon become fixed, narrow and repetitive.

One woman described a life that had become a regimented nightmare that revolved around the clock. Getting up, mealtimes and going to bed: her whole life was organised and controlled. How had it become this way? It appeared that when they first married she had tried very hard to please her husband and had allowed him the control of the daily running of the house. She did not realise that once these routines became fixed she would be unlikely to get him to change them. It is very important not to allow strict routines to develop in the relationship, as once established, trying to change them may cause a lot of stress and anxiety.

When routines are a problem

If family life is totally regimented by routines, the whole family may feel very controlled, and life can feel as though nothing is ever spontaneous or fun.

If your relationship is relatively new, then start as you mean to go on. So, if there is something your partner is doing that you really cannot stand, try to stop it before it develops into a set pattern.

If the routine is already established, however, it may be very difficult or even sometimes impossible to change completely.

Small changes are sometimes possible if the non-Asperger partner is willing to stand their ground. For example, one woman's Asperger husband insisted that no one was allowed to speak while they sat at the dinner table: meals had to be in absolute silence. Mealtimes for the woman and the children became very stressful and not an enjoyable experience. The woman told her husband that unless he was more lenient, they would all eat at separate times. This did not work, so she told him that in future he would have to get his own dinner. He then agreed to compromise, and it was decided that they would not talk while eating but could talk before, after or in between courses. It was a small compromise and she had to be very firm and stand by her threat, but it achieved a change and helped alleviate some of the pressure on the relationship.

Another way that may prove helpful in tolerating routines is to look for the positive. One man described how his Asperger partner was obsessive about the sponges they used to wash up. She would insist that yellow ones were for washing up crockery, green ones for cooking utensils and blue ones for wiping surfaces. Trying to remember which was which drove him to distraction, yet when she went away to stay with her sister, he found himself following the same routine. In doing so, he saw some logic in it. Since then, his partner's habit has no longer irritated him, and he even made a list and put it above the sink to remind him of her colour code.

Routines can be useful

Most men and women I have spoken to talked about their partner's routines in favourable terms. Some said it was a relief that they never had to check the house was locked up at night and always knew the bath would be clean. One woman's partner always did their own ironing so that this could be done their way, which she was definitely very happy about.

A perfect job

Adults with Asperger syndrome can be very dependable and, if given something to do, as long as they want to do it, they will do it no matter what. They will complete the job and it will be done to perfection. It may take them a while – and you will have to be patient as they will not take short-cuts or 'make do' – but the result will be worth it.

Different people with Asperger syndrome are gifted in different ways. One woman described how her partner mapped out all her routes for her and, even though she had to sit with him for ages while he described every landmark on the way, she knew she would not get lost and would be grateful later for the comfort of knowing exactly where she was going.

20

SOCIALISING SOLUTIONS

Social problems

Many women told me about problems that had occurred in social situations that at times made life very difficult. Sometimes people with Asperger syndrome (Autism Spectrum Disorder) will do anything to avoid such events. Having problems with knowing how to interact socially with others is one of the core traits of Asperger syndrome, so it is inevitable that, some way or another, this area will be a challenge for your relationship. The exact problems, though, will vary from couple to couple, so the degree of disruption and inconvenience they cause will also vary.

The introvert

Most adults with Asperger syndrome seem to either display introvert or extrovert traits; the majority, however, appear to be quite introvert by nature, and introverts will go to any lengths to avoid social situations. For example, some Asperger partners quite simply refuse to socialise at all – some don't come home from work when they know that some event has been arranged or, if they do attend, they may fall asleep or be so rude to other people that their partner may wish they had not come. Some have found themselves getting a taxi home as their partners have left them alone at a social gathering, disappearing altogether without any prior warning.

The extrovert

As well as the Asperger partners who avoid social situations, there are a few who go to the other extreme and behave in an extrovert way, especially if they have had a drink. They may become quite loud and overpowering, often making jokes that no one understands, which can cause a lot of embarrassment for their non-Asperger partners. It may appear that their behaviour is reverting to that of adolescence, and they are unaware of how they appear to others. Alternatively, they may start talking about their favourite hobby and some poor unsuspecting person becomes trapped in a one-way conversation (this can apply to both introverts and extroverts).

Getting on better with the other sex

If your Asperger partner is male, then he may have a highly developed feminine side, and so will often appear to get on better with women than men. This may be because other boys bullied him at school, which sadly happens to many boys with Asperger syndrome. Your partner may find women are more tolerant of his lack of confidence and conversational topics, and he would have learned quickly that he is more likely to be accepted by females than males.

Interestingly, I found that this was also the case for the women with the syndrome whom I contacted, but in reverse, as they showed a preference for male friends. One woman with Asperger syndrome described to me the difficulty she had in conversing with women. She said she found most women quite boring! Her topic of conversation with other women was quite restricted.

One of the reasons females with Asperger syndrome may find that males are easier to get on with is because they make fewer emotional demands on them.

Inappropriate flirting

Sometimes those with Asperger syndrome can become quite fixed on one particular person, say, at a party. If this person is of the opposite sex, this may create mixed messages. They may stand too close to the other person or disclose too much information for just a casual chat. This may look like blatant and inappropriate flirting. Unless the non-Asperger partner recognises what is happening quite quickly, and tactfully interrupts and leads their partner away, it could cause upset and misunderstandings for all those involved.

Literal interpretation

Taking things literally and not understanding jokes and sarcasm can make socialising a nightmare for someone with Asperger syndrome. The women I contacted in the course of my original research gave accounts of some very awkward situations that arose because of their partner's misinterpretation of what someone said, or not knowing when something was a joke. For instance, one woman described a time at a party when her partner was asked jokingly where he was 'coming from'. This completely confused him, and when he answered, very seriously, that he had just come from the toilet, everyone laughed. Her husband did not understand what he had said that was so funny.

Likewise, not realising that honesty is not always the best policy when asked to give an opinion can cause problems. People with Asperger syndrome will inevitably give a very honest answer, and sometimes this will cause offence.

Exaggerations

Exaggeration forms part of our daily communication and we are often not aware we are even doing it. For example, we may say it rained for weeks when in fact it only rained for a couple of days, or we may say a journey took us all day, when it took only three hours. We accept these exaggerations and know that the queue for the checkout was not miles long, and that there were not hundreds of people waiting for the bus.

Your partner with Asperger syndrome may not know you are exaggerating, and it is important that you tell them things as they really are. One woman had complained to her Asperger partner that her nail varnish took hours to dry and he discussed this with the receptionist at his workplace, seriously convinced that his wife had told him the truth. The receptionist was unable to tell him that this was not normally the case and was probably left thinking that the whole conversation was rather bizarre.

Your Asperger partner will not understand exaggerations, and to avoid embarrassment for both of you, be aware that what you are saying is based on facts.

Not recognising the dangers

Another problem that was described by some of the men and women I spoke to was their partner's difficulty in recognising potentially dangerous situations. This may be due to not reading the signals, or because their partner had become focused on one particular thing. A situation described to me by one woman took place in the car park of a well-known drive-in burger restaurant. Her husband noticed a group of rather rowdy men in a car throw all their empty cartons into the car park. Her husband got out of the car, walked over to the men's car, picked up their rubbish and chucked it back through their car window, with the comment that he believed it to be theirs. He brushed his hands together and walked back to his car, got in and drove away, luckily before they were able to react. It may seem that he was being very brave and standing up for his beliefs, but it is more likely that he did not recognise the potential danger that he was putting both himself and his family into.

Men have described similar incidents, especially when their Asperger partners have not recognised that a man was coming on to them and they have unintentionally given them all the wrong signals. One young man in his twenties described how at a social event his Asperger partner was talking to a male work colleague and it was when he became aware that she was missing that he realised something was amiss. When he found her outside trying to break away from the unwanted advances of the male work colleague he was very angry with the man, and equally upset with his partner. Luckily he understood Asperger syndrome and knew too well that his partner did not always read other people's intentions – when her work colleague had suggested they go outside for a breath of fresh air, she had grabbed the opportunity to escape for a while. She was totally unaware that to this man it meant she was interested in him. After this they made it a rule to not be separated at social events.

Difficulty transferring information

Often those with Asperger syndrome do not have the ability to transfer information from one situation to another. It is possible for your partner to learn that it is impolite to make comments on what a person is wearing, even if it really does not suit them, but what about when you want your partner's real opinion about something important? They will probably just agree with whatever is being said and leave you to make the decision alone rather than run the risk of saying the wrong thing. This example may sound quite trivial, but in fact, it is things like this that cause tension. You may feel that you are left with all the responsibility and that you do not know if your partner agrees with you or not. If you tell your partner that you will not get angry or upset if they tell you the truth about something, it is vital that you see this promise through, whatever the answer. If you do not do this, your partner will remember your reaction and probably be very reluctant to tell the truth again.

Thinking ahead

Unless your Asperger partner refuses to socialise under any circumstances, there is nothing to say that they cannot be helped to get through the social situations that are causing problems. You will, over time, probably develop a sixth sense for when you need to intervene to save a situation. You may, for example, notice that your partner has been talking for too long to a polite guest, who is slowly learning all there is to know about your partner's pet subject. If you are planning to eat out, check in advance that the restaurant passes the 'Asperger test' – that is, it is very clean and has a selection of food that you both enjoy. Thinking ahead is always a useful strategy – prevention is better than cure.

If you know in advance that you are going to be in the company of people who are sensitive to particular issues or hold very strong beliefs or opinions, talk to your partner first and explain the subjects that are taboo and that would be best left alone. Your partner will often not realise that sometimes their sense of humour or honesty may be very upsetting for someone else. The sense of humour of an adult with Asperger syndrome can often be very adolescent in nature. Sometimes jokes are repetitive and therefore become irritating rather than funny. One man I spoke to who had Asperger syndrome always made rhymes out of people's names, which were not always complimentary: I never asked what his rhyme was for my name!

Many difficult situations have been described to me over the years. One woman described how her husband made jokes about body bags while visiting her mother in hospital, where she had just had a major operation. Another woman explained her utter disbelief when her husband told one of their friends that she smelled. No one knew what to say and all just stood in complete silence. Luckily his wife was able to brush it aside by telling her friend not to worry because he said that to her all the time, and it just meant that they must be wearing the same perfume. With that, she grabbed her husband by the arm and marched him off.

Situations like this can be embarrassing and sometimes very hurtful for others. In time you will become more aware of certain tricky situations and the areas of conversation to avoid. You will be able to brief your partner on what not to say, and what subjects not to mention such as religion, politics or morals, to name but a few.

A single focus

A feature of Asperger syndrome is that of becoming quite stuck and focused on one particular object or subject. One woman described how her husband always seemed to become obsessed with the seating arrangements whenever they went out for a meal. He saw it as his duty to make certain everyone sat in the order he found appropriate, which normally placed him as far away from the children as possible. He would achieve this even if it involved the entire family having to get up and move around the table. At times like this his wife decided it was easier to let him just get on with it rather than cause a fuss in a public place. He would only have argued that he was just trying to look after everyone and that he was acting in their best interests.

Always doing their best

It may be helpful to allocate something useful for your partner to do on social occasions. If you are having a party, ask them to take care of the drinks, the food or, better still, the music. You can guarantee that your partner will soon have the CDs completely organised and, although everyone will have to spend the entire evening listening to their choice of music, it will be sorted out and you will not have to worry about it.

A word of warning, though: think carefully about the tasks that you give to your partner as they will take them very seriously and not stop until their mission is completed. One woman told me about a fireworks display that the entire family, including aunts and uncles, went to one bonfire night. It was taking place in the grounds of an old castle. She asked her husband, who was more familiar with the layout of the castle grounds than she was, if he could find the best possible place for them to stand to see the fireworks. He certainly found the best place, but the effort it took to get there was quite traumatising, climbing over rocks and down slippery slopes, all at a rate of knots, with her husband rushing ahead like a squadron leader, ordering everyone around.

By the time the family got there, no one was in the right frame of mind to enjoy the display – two family members had walked off and the poor wife was a complete nervous wreck.

Your partner's determination to complete a task can, therefore, be a bonus, but only if it is channelled in the right direction. This seems more relevant for men with Asperger syndrome than women, as women tend to be more inclined to stay in the background and allow their partner to take the limelight; this cannot be applied to all women on the spectrum, however.

The deserter

If, while entertaining, your partner wants to go to another room and look through their favourite magazines or go for a walk or to bed, does it really matter? They have not really deserted or abandoned you, and will have given as much time as they can manage. Maybe socialising is not their thing, and it was probably not their choice to be in this social situation in the first place.

If friends know that your partner has Asperger syndrome, then they will understand that socialising is difficult for them and often time-limited. If they do not know, then they can be told that your partner is very tired or feeling unwell. One man described how he became aware that whenever they went to a social event or works do, his Asperger wife would disappear, for rather a long time, into the ladies toilet. The first time this happened he became quite concerned when she had been missing for almost 15 minutes, and sent someone in to look for her. This was quite embarrassing for his wife and she was very annoyed with him. This was, however, before they were aware of Asperger syndrome; now he understands it has become part of the evening schedule and he helps his wife choose appropriate moments for time out, and has a list of excuses he can use to explain her absence.

Many men and women have become experts at making excuses for their Asperger partners and covering up for them.

Unfortunately, however, your partner may not appreciate how hard you try to smooth things over for them. They may not show any empathy for the sacrifices that you have made for them, which can make it hard to bear. Is this part of Asperger syndrome or is your partner just being selfish? The next chapter answers this question.

21

EMPATHY AND RECIPROCITY

Lack of empathy

Empathy is the ability to put yourself in someone else's shoes. It is important not to confuse it with sympathy, as individuals with Asperger syndrome (Autistic Spectrum Disorder) are able to show much sympathy. Having a lack of empathy is one of the aspects of Asperger syndrome that non-Asperger partners find hardest to deal with. This problem is intensified because not empathising means that partners are unlikely to be appreciated for all the effort, time and self-sacrifice they have to put into the relationship because of the presence of the syndrome.

Your partner is unlikely to be upset because they have upset you, but will be upset if your reaction to something affects their routine or interferes with the way they are treated. It is easier for both of you if you know that this lack of empathy and appreciation for your efforts is not your partner being intentionally hurtful. They are not holding anything back – they are probably unaware of what they should do or feel grateful for. Indeed, they are unlikely to have any idea what it is that you are getting so upset and stressed about.

Adults with Asperger syndrome are just being themselves and doing things in their own way, and do not have any particular problems with the way they are. They may see their partner as being the one with the problem, the one who complains and moans all the time. Because of difficulties applying empathy, they may not be able to see that the problem their partner has stems from something to do with their own behaviour.

It is important to understand that a lack of empathy does not mean your partner cannot ever understand things from your perspective. If the situation is calm and things are going well, empathy can be shown when the non-Asperger partner is able to explain their viewpoint in a way that is logical and non-emotional.

Asperger syndrome, or just being selfish?

The behaviour of those with Asperger syndrome can appear very selfish, but this is part and parcel of the condition, and they are probably not even aware that what they are doing is sometimes very one-sided. They may expect their daily routine to remain unchanged or for you to be interested and to listen patiently when they are trying to tell you something about their special interest. They may also insist that you do certain things the way they want them to be done.

It sounds like the ultimate in selfishness that the only needs they are bothered about are their own, but in fact, it is simply that they are unaware of how some things they do come across to others. Their behaviour is a consequence of Asperger syndrome, which means they have difficulty conceptualising how others may feel and are unable to put themselves in someone else's shoes. This does not mean that they do not care or feel concern for you, but that they are not able to imagine what you may be feeling.

Reciprocity means to feel or give in return for the same. Most relationships depend on reciprocity to make them work – there has to be give and take. Some men and women I have come into contact with felt that they gave while their partners took.

However, no amount of nagging, bribing, emotional blackmail or ultimatums will make any difference. These will just put your partner under tremendous pressure because they do not know how to show or express this thing you call empathy in the way you would wish it.

For the relationship to continue less stressfully, maintain a realistic view of the situation and do not strive for the impossible. Your partner cannot give you something they do not have, but they can protect you, care, show concern and give comfort if they are made aware that this is what is required of them.

Externalising the blame

One of the ways in which some men and women coped in such a non-reciprocal relationship was by externalising all their partner's negative traits, blaming them on Asperger syndrome. They blamed the syndrome as if it were a third party and could then live with their partner's behaviour. Sometimes this may make the difference between continuing in the relationship or not.

For example, a man whose Asperger wife was training to become a lawyer was due to take her final exams when she took a call from the local hospital to say that her husband's brother-in-law had passed away after a long-term illness. She made the decision not to pass on the message until after her exams as she did not want the incident to affect her schedule for the day. When her husband found out, he was furious and felt very let down by his wife. He challenged her and she informed him that she had felt there was little point telling him as his brother had already passed away and there was nothing he could do. This information made matters even worse, and it was only when someone told him they thought his wife might be on the autism spectrum that everything started to make sense. He discussed this with her and they went together for an assessment, where she received a positive diagnosis. This changed everything and he could now see things very differently and was able to make sense of his wife's actions, which, when viewed through a different lens, seemed logical rather than uncaring.

Externalisation of blame is not unusual – it is a way of dealing with the flaws our loved ones have. Often when things go wrong for people, such as failing at a task, they blame all manner of things, from lack of time to the weather. The fact, then, that so many men and women blame Asperger syndrome for everything negative about their partner is not so unusual. It is, in fact, a brilliant strategy and it really works. Remember, though, that there are many things your partner can make choices about, just like anyone else.

22

ASPERGER SYNDROME (AUTISM SPECTRUM DISORDER) CANNOT BE BLAMED FOR EVERYTHING

Just because your partner has Asperger syndrome does not mean that they have no choice but to do what they do in all areas of their life. It is not an excuse to be violent, aggressive, verbally abusive or a control freak; it is not an excuse to gamble; nor is it an excuse to be unfaithful. There are many rules and boundaries within any relationship that have to be respected, and in no way should anyone tolerate anything that they feel puts them or their children in danger or causes them extreme stress or heartbreak.

In all close relationships, whether Asperger syndrome is present or not, each partner has to decide what they are and are not prepared to tolerate. Certainly, if someone with Asperger syndrome is capable of forming an intimate relationship, they should also be quite capable of knowing that there are some types of behaviour that are totally unacceptable and inappropriate, and top of the list is domestic violence.

Domestic violence

Having Asperger syndrome is not an excuse to be physically violent or aggressive towards you or your children, and should not be tolerated in any circumstances, regardless of whether you are male or female. And having the syndrome does not mean that your partner is more likely to be violent or aggressive – in fact, evidence from the women I have contacted and my work suggests that physical violence appears to be quite uncommon.

Anger also seems to be quite short-lived, and can make its appearance in the form of a sudden outburst. There may be a build-up of daily hassles and then something seemingly irrelevant triggers explosive anger, which may be quite out of character and frightening. Some men and women said that their partner throws or breaks the nearest object to hand. Usually it is only the object that gets physically damaged, but what about the damage this can do to their partner's emotional well-being?

Anger without a cause

What follows does not apply to all adults with Asperger syndrome as not all of them have sudden bursts of anger. If your partner is someone who does have such outbursts, you may be left wondering what you said or did to cause it, as this reaction seems to come out of the blue and is often over something seemingly trivial.

Asperger anger seems to be sharp and very short-lived, so it will disperse as quickly as it appeared. Afterwards, your partner will be fine again and you will often be left wondering why they were so upset. You will feel wounded, attacked and probably in a flood of tears, while your partner will not understand what is wrong and may expect you to recover as quickly as they have. They will just want to get on with their day and for you to carry on as before and not disrupt any plans. It is you who will be left to deal with the aftermath alone.

After an argument

After an argument it is helpful to have someone you can talk to who understands how you feel – maybe someone in the family or, even better, someone else who has a partner with Asperger syndrome. Talking is therapeutic, which is why counselling can be so useful. When things have calmed down, maybe you can discuss the incident with your partner using the golden rules of Asperger syndrome communication mentioned earlier.

One couple found that letter writing worked best for them if the woman felt hurt or upset by something her partner had done or said. She would write him a letter and leave it somewhere for him to find. This allowed him to sit quietly and read what she had written. He would then email her from work or write her a note back. This way both could say what they wanted without being interrupted. This worked for them, but another way may work better for you.

Displaced anger

Sometimes it turns out that the angry outburst is not about you at all, which explains why it seems to come from nowhere, and the feeling that it does not relate to anything you were talking about or doing at the time. One woman described just such an incident. She had asked her husband to pick up a newspaper on the way home from work. When he arrived home and had forgotten it, she said in a half humorous way that he could not be depended on for anything, and she would not ask him again. He 'went up in the air like a rocket', picked up a chair and broke it. The children ran into the room as they were so concerned, and, without speaking, her husband stormed out of the house. She just stood there amazed. She felt that she was the one who should have been angry and was very upset by the whole episode. Her husband returned home later, but would not discuss the incident. It was only the next day, when she spoke to a friend who worked with him, that she discovered he had had a really bad day at work. He had complained that some of the other men were not pulling their weight and spent more time reading the newspaper than doing their work.

It is clear from this that he had contained his anger at work, ignoring it when workmates had made some pretty cruel remarks to him, but he had internalised the negative effect of the whole episode. The anger he unleashed as a reaction to what his wife said belonged with the men at work, but his wife got the whole lot, and all because he thought she was 'running him down'. He was, sadly, unable to detach one situation from another, and placed her in the same category as the men back on the shop floor.

Such incidents are not uncommon if your partner has Asperger syndrome, so it is always a good idea to look deeper into any situation. You may not always find a reason, but it is worth checking things out because you may just get to the bottom of it.

What about verbal abuse?

Physical violence was rarely reported among the women I contacted in my original research, and this has remained unchanged after working with hundreds of couples over many years. Sometimes, though, the abuse is verbal, and words can be used in an abusive way and hurt as much as physical abuse.

Verbal abuse can wreck a person's self-esteem and feelings of self-worth. Episodes of verbal abuse were reported in some of the relationships and, among these, some said this happened quite frequently. Unfortunately, once a pattern of verbal abuse has been established within a couple, it can be very hard to break. This may be even more the case when the abusive partner has Asperger syndrome.

Some change can be achieved if the partner with Asperger syndrome has enough incentive to do something about it. If you are on the receiving end of such abuse, you must decide what you are prepared to accept and will not accept.

Being objective

Choose an appropriate moment and try to discuss with your partner how what they are saying makes you feel. Alternatively, try writing to your partner if you feel this would have a better effect. You could make up a list of words that are not acceptable as well as a list of alternative harmless words, and ask your partner also to draw up such lists.

If possible, try to discuss things in an objective way, remaining neutral and practical. Try negotiating by saying, 'When you say this to me, it makes me upset. If I am upset I cannot cook your dinner, or I cannot talk to you about [special interest]. I would be much happier if you would not say...'

It is important not to blame or criticise. Your partner also needs to know when what they are saying and doing is all right, perhaps even great, and how happy it makes you when they do this or say that. You should both try to keep in mind the positives about each other and the relationship you share.

Tight boundaries

It is important that your partner knows how their behaviour makes you feel. Always try to talk about the things that bother you and do not cover up for any behaviour that is in any way abusive as this will give your partner the message that it is okay to behave in this way. This seems to be more difficult for men with an Asperger partner who is female – they will sometimes ignore or just distance themselves from their partner rather than discuss the issues with them.

It is not wise to think that your partner just needs to get things out of their system as they could interpret this as being given permission to continue what they are doing. The boundaries must be kept tight, with no fuzzy edges. People with Asperger syndrome need rules and boundaries because they do not always automatically know what is required of them, either in a social, emotional or intimate situation.

Being clear and precise

Always make sure that your partner knows exactly which types of behaviour are completely unacceptable and, if possible, let them know this right from the start of the relationship. They need to be told what is not acceptable and that the relationship will be at severe risk or, if necessary, finished if they cross these boundaries.

For those with Asperger syndrome, rules and boundaries must be very clear and precise. Don't take it for granted that your partner will understand automatically from the beginning what is acceptable and what is not. Much will depend on their own parental role models and what kind of upbringing they had, as habits and messages that Asperger syndrome children pick up at an early age can be very difficult to challenge and change later on.

The importance of early diagnosis

If you met your partner at a relatively young age and recognised quite soon that they had Asperger syndrome, or if a positive diagnosis was given early on and your partner received the help and guidance required, then there is a far better chance of making your relationship work and being able to compromise and negotiate together.

If, however, the diagnosis was not made until later on, possibly with a failed marriage or abusive relationship already behind them, it will be more difficult to change things because your partner will already be quite set in their ways and will have developed set routines. They may have developed certain 'scripts' and patterns for different situations – even a very set script for what constitutes a 'wife' or 'husband' or 'civil partner'. This may be based on their experience of how their mother and father played out their relationship with them, something they had read or watched on television, or maybe their relationship with a previous partner. Bringing about change in these circumstances can be harder but, with an awareness of what is causing the difficulties and an incentive to try to change things, the relationship can still improve.

23

STAYING TOGETHER

The positive sides of Asperger syndrome (Autism Spectrum Disorder)

Many of the men and women I have encountered attribute all the positive qualities their partner displays to their own individual personality. For some women the main plus point they mention is their partner's gentleness – they feel safe in the knowledge that their partner is unlikely ever to become violent or to hurt them. Others said that they were pleased that their partner was not 'one of the boys', did not 'live in the pub' and come in drunk at night. They liked the fact that their partner was far happier to stay in at home, watching television or working on the house. For both non-Asperger men and women, the most positive things about their partners were, first, their interesting and fascinating minds – they admired how their partners could think outside the box and offer a very different perspective on life; and second, they admired their partners' faithfulness and lack of sexual interest they showed in others. This made them feel secure, and being able to relax and be themselves rather than feeling threatened by other men and women was a great bonus.

Things can get better, in time

It does seem that people with Asperger syndrome improve with age and, with time, the negative aspects of the syndrome may lessen. This could be because they are able to learn more about what their partner wants and does not want. They also want a quiet life, and this need probably increases as they get older, so they learn that if they do 'x', 'y' will happen. This does not mean they are getting over Asperger syndrome, just that they are learning strategies to avoid annoying anyone and making their life with their partner easier. It may also be that their partner is becoming more familiar with the syndrome, and possibly echoing some Asperger traits themselves. Although it might seem as if this would make the relationship more manageable, however, it may leave the partner feeling that they have lost a part of themselves.

Taking on Asperger traits

If, after a period of time, you start to wonder if you have Asperger syndrome yourself, or are developing certain Asperger traits, then think seriously what you are going to do about it, as you could end up feeling that you have lost your individuality or your 'self'. Having a sense of self is important for any individual who wishes to remain an individual, so this could be a sign that you need to start doing more for yourself, or spending more time in the company of those who do not have Asperger syndrome. If you do not have many friends, then you could take up a hobby that involves others, such as art classes, playing squash or a part-time course. You could take a short break with a good friend, or your children. Whatever you decide on, you should come into contact with other people who do not have Asperger syndrome.

Self-help

Many of the men and women in a relationship with someone with Asperger syndrome display a strong ability to make changes in their lives in order to improve things for themselves. Some go to counselling or seek some other form of therapeutic help, for example, yoga, sport or an exercise class. Others may take up some form of studying, enrolling at their local college or university as mature students, and may discover that they have talents they did not know existed. One man discovered his talent for photography and now makes money out of it. Many are able to create a support system and live for themselves outside the relationship so that they do not depend solely on their partner for emotional support, which they have realised their partner is unable to give them.

All of the women I contacted in my original research, and many of the men and women I have come into contact since, have, in some way, taken control of their situation and done something positive about it. If you are in this situation, then you are also doing something positive about your situation by reading this book.

If one of you decides to leave

It would be quite unusual for your Asperger partner to be the one to walk out on the relationship. If they did decide to leave, however, it would be a rare thing if they came back, and if they did, it would probably be on their terms with you as the one to make most of the changes.

If, however, your partner with Asperger syndrome does leave, clearly this can be devastating, leaving you in a state of shock, wondering how they could do this to you when you have tried so hard. It could be helpful at this time to find a counsellor who understands and can help you through this difficult time.

It could be equally devastating for a partner with Asperger syndrome to be abandoned, and many men and women expressed the concern that they felt their partners would not be able to cope without them. Everyone has choices, however. We can decide to stay in a relationship or leave. It is not enough to stay for the sake of the children or for financial reasons or because one partner has become dependent on the other if the cost is a loss of well-being, self-esteem and even health.

Your partner with Asperger syndrome can give a lot, but there are some things they will not be able to give. And while there are some ways in which they can change, there are also some things they will not be able to change. They are quite capable of loving someone, but may not be very good at showing or expressing it. Neither will they always be able to offer suitable emotional support or make you feel understood and that you are receiving adequate empathy.

Some men and women reported feeling that their partner's love for them felt more like a need, that they felt important to them for many reasons, but not because their partner needed a soul mate who could share their deepest feelings and most intimate moments and secrets. It is quite possible to feel that you are needed in the same way that a walking stick is needed by someone who has a limp – making your partner's journey through life easier, safer and more comfortable.

Your partner will want you to share their time and special interests. Their need for you is of a very practical and necessary nature, but in return they can offer you the kind of loyalty that is consistent and unique.

A special kind of security

Your partner may offer you a special kind of security that, in these days of high rates of divorce and separation, is very hard to find. They will probably stick by you for all of your life. They are very likely to work hard and take care of what they are able to.

Most of the partners with Asperger syndrome whom I interviewed and have encountered since showed a strong commitment to their relationships and offered a sincere faithfulness. Those with Asperger syndrome who are committed and hardworking individuals are generally loyal and long-term partners.

You must decide what is most important to you. Maybe it is best if you think of your partner as having a disability, and that it is this disability that restricts them in some areas of social interaction, communication and empathetic and imaginative thought, but that it does not alter the kind of person they are – their morals, level of commitment to the relationship, whether or not they are violent or abusive to you or your children, or if they are faithful or not. Your decision to stay or not to stay should be based on your partner's personality and the things that your partner can make their own decisions about, not just the fact that they have Asperger syndrome.

USEFUL SOURCES OF HELP
AND INFORMATION

Asperger's Association of New England (AANE) (www.aane.org), a website for spouses of partners with Asperger syndrome. It offers understanding and support for the non-Asperger partner.

Aspergers And Other Half (http://groups.yahoo.com/neo/groups/ AspergersAndOtherHalf/info) is for partners/spouses (females only) of individuals suspected to have, or officially diagnosed with, Asperger syndrome, to connect with other women facing similar situations who understand the realities of relationships with a partner on the spectrum. It is a safe place for women to talk about their experiences without facing disbelief, finding people who are familiar with their experiences and who offer empathy and support.

Asperger Syndrome Partners and Individuals Resources, Encouragement and Support (ASPIRES) (www.aspires-relation ships.com), an online resource for spouses and family members of adults diagnosed or suspected to be on the autistm spectrum. Approaches to one another and towards 'significant others' are directed towards solving problems in the relationship with a spectrum-sitting spouse.

Relate Derby and Southern Derbyshire (http://relatederby.org. uk) enables people to talk directly to a counsellor and to discuss, in confidence, any relationship issues they have regarding Asperger syndrome. All calls to the Derby Relate Line are charged at the standard national rate. Address: 62 Friar Gate, Derby DE1 1DJ; Tel: 01332 349177 [lines open every Tuesday, 10.30am until 4.30pm]; Email: info@relatederby.org.uk; Twitter: @RelateDerby

Families of Adults Afflicted by Asperger's Syndrome (FAAAS) (www.faaas.org) is run by Karen E. Rodman, whose husband has both Asperger and Tourette's syndromes. It is for the non-Asperger partner.

The National Autistic Society (www.autism.org.uk) is the leading UK charity for people with autism (including Asperger syndrome)

and their families, providing information and support for people on the autism spectrum.

Online Asperger Syndrome Information and Support (OASIS @ MAPP) (www.aspergersyndrome.org), a single resource for families and medical professionals dealing with the challenges of Asperger syndrome, autism and pervasive developmental disorder/not otherwise specified (PDD/NOS).

Asperger Partner (www.aspergerpartner.dk), a Danish neurotypical site with some articles in English.

Professor Tony Attwood (www.tonyattwood.com), a well respected author and expert on the subject of Asperger syndrome, especially as it relates to personal relationships and family dynamics.

REFERENCES

APA (American Psychiatric Association) (1994) *Diagnostic and Statistical Manual of Mental Disorders* (4th edn). Washington, DC: APA.

APA (2013) *Diagnostic and Statistical Manual of Mental Disorders* (5th edn). Washington, DC: APA.

Asperger, H. (1944) 'Die "Autistischen Psychopath". *Kindesalter, Archiv für psychiatrie und nervenkrankheiten 117*, 76–136. Reprinted in U. Frith (1991) *Autism and Asperger Syndrome*. Cambridge: Cambridge University Press.

Attwood, T. (1998) *Asperger's Syndrome: A Guide for Parents and Professionals*. London: Jessica Kingsley Publishers.

Bailey, A., Le Couteur, A., Gottesman, I., Bolton, P., Simonoff, E., Yuzda, E. and Rutter, M. (1995) 'Autism as a strongly genetic disorder: evidence from a British twin study.' *Psychological Medicine 25*, 63–77.

Baird, G., Simonoff, E., Pickles, A., Chandler, S., Loucas, T., Meldrum, D. and Charman, T. (2006) 'Prevalence of disorders of the autism spectrum in a population cohort of children in South Thames: the Special Needs and Autism Project (SNAP).' *The Lancet 368*, 9531, 210–215.

Baron-Cohen, S. and Wheelwright, C.S. (1999) '"Obsessions" in children with Autism or Asperger syndrome.' *British Journal of Psychiatry 175*, 484–490.

Baron-Cohen, S., Wheelwright, S., Stott, C., Bolton, P. and Goodyer, I. (1997) 'Is there a link between engineering and autism?' *Autism 1*, 101–109.

Brugha, T.S., McManus, S., Bankart, J., Scott, F., Purdon, S., Smith, J., Bebbington, P., Jenkins, R. and Meltzer, H. (2009) *Autism Spectrum Disorders in Adults Living in Households throughout England: Report from the Adult Psychiatric Morbidity Survey, 2007*. Leeds: NHS Information Centre for Health and Social Care.

Brugha, T.S, McManus, S., Bankart, J., Scott, F., Purdon, S., Smith, J. *et al.* (2011) 'Epidemiology of autism spectrum disorders in adults in the community in England.' *Archives of General Psychiatry 68*, 5, May, 459–465.

Brugha, T.S., McManus, S., Smith, J., Scott, F.J., Meltzer, H., Purdon, S., Berney, T., Tantam, D., Robinson, J., Radley, J. and Bankart, J. (2012) 'Validating two survey methods for identifying cases of autism spectrum disorder among adults in the community.' *Psychological Medicine 42*, 3, March, 647–656.

Burgoine, E. and Wing, L. (1983) 'Identical triplets with Asperger's syndrome.' *British Journal of Psychiatry 143*, 261–265.

CDCP (Centers for Disease Control and Prevention) (2001) *Utilization of Ambulatory Medical Care by Women: United States, 1997–98 Vital and Health Statistics*, Series 13, Number 149. Available at www.cdc.gov/nchs/data/series/sr_13/sr13_149.pdf, accessed on 19 July 2003.

Ehlers, S. and Gillberg, C. (1993) 'The epidemiology of Asperger syndrome: A total population study.' *Journal of Child Psychology and Psychiatry 34*, 1327–1350.

Folstein, S.E. and Rosen-Sheidley, B. (2001) 'Genetics of autism: complex aetiology for a heterogeneous disorder.' *Macmillan Magazines Ltd 2*, December, 943–955.

Folstein, S.E., Bisson, E., Santangelo, S.L. and Piven, J. (1998) 'Finding specific genes that cause Autism: a combination of approaches will be needed to maximize power.' *Journal of Autism and Developmental Disorders 28*, 5, 439–445.

Gillberg, C. (1989) 'Asperger syndrome in 23 Swedish children.' *Developmental Medicine and Child Neurology 31*, 520–531.

Golan, O., Baron-Cohen, S. and Hill. J. (2006) 'The Cambridge Mindreading (CAM) Face-Voice Battery: testing complex emotion recognition in adults with and without Asperger syndrome.' *Journal of Autism Developmental Disorders 36*, 2, February, 169–183.

Holliday Willey, L. (1999) *Pretending to be Normal*. London: Jessica Kingsley Publishers.

Holliday Willey, L. and Attwood, T. (2000) *Asperger's Syndrome – Crossing the Bridge*. Michael Thompson Productions [video].

Kadesjö, B., Gillberg, C. and Hagberg, B. (1999) 'Brief report: autism and Asperger syndrome in seven-year-old children: a total population study.' *Journal of Autism and Developmental Disorders 29*, 4, 327–331.

Montagne, B., Kessels, R.P., Frigerio, E., de Haan, E.H. and Perrett, D.I. (2005) 'Sex differences in the perception of affective facial expressions: do men really lack emotional sensitivity?' *Cognitive Processing 6*, 2, June, 136–141.

Noller, P. (1980) 'Misunderstandings in marital communication: a study of couples' non-verbal communication.' *Journal of Personality and Social Psychology 39*, 1135–1148.

Schopler, E., Mesibov, G.B. and Kunce, L.J. (1998) *Asperger Syndrome or High-Functioning Autism?* New York and London: Plenum Press.

Simone, R. (2010) *Aspergirls: Empowering Females with Asperger Syndrome*. London: Jessica Kingsley Publishers.

Then, D. (1997) *Women Who Stay with Men Who Stray*. London: Thorsons.

Volkmar, F.R., Klin, A. and Pauls, D. (1998) 'Nosological and genetic aspects of Asperger syndrome.' *Journal of Autism and Development Disorders 28*, 5, October, 457–463.

Wing, L. (1981) 'Asperger's Syndrome: a clinical account.' *Psychological Medicine 11*, 115–130.

FURTHER READING

Aston, M.C. (2003) *Aspergers in Love: Couple Relationships and Family Affairs.* London: Jessica Kingsley Publishers.

Aston, M.C. (2008) *The Asperger Couples Workbook.* London: Jessica Kingsley Publishers.

Aston, M.C. (2012) *What Men with Asperger's Want To Know about Women, Dating and Relationships.* London: Jessica Kingsley Publishers.

Attwood, T. (2007) *The Complete Guide to Asperger's Syndrome.* London: Jessica Kingsley Publishers.

Baron-Cohen, S. (1997) *Mindblindness: An Essay on Autism and Theory of Mind.* London: MIT Press.

Bentley. K. (2007) *Alone Together: Making an Asperger Marriage Work.* London: Jessica Kingsley Publishers.

Frith, U. (ed.) (1991) *Autism and Asperger Syndrome.* Cambridge: Cambridge University Press.

Hendrickx, S. (2008) *Love, Sex and Long-Term Relationships.* London: Jessica Kingsley Publishers.

Hendrickx, S. and Newton, K. (2007) *Asperger Syndrome – A Love Story.* London: Jessica Kingsley Publishers.

Holliday Willey, L. (2001) *Asperger's Syndrome in the Family.* London: Jessica Kingsley Publishers.

Rodman, K. (2003) *Asperger's Syndrome and Adults... Is Anyone Listening? Essays and Poems by Partners, Parents and Family Members.* London: Jessica Kingsley Publishers.

Simone, R. (2009) *22 Things a Woman Must Know If She Loves a Man with Asperger's Syndrome.* London: Jessica Kingsley Publishers.

Tantam, D. and Prestwood, S. (1999) *A Mind of One's Own* (3rd edn). London: The National Autistic Society.

Weston, L. (2010) *Connecting with Your Asperger Partner: Negotiating the Maze of Intimacy.* London: Jessica Kingsley Publishers.

Wing, L. (1996) *The Autistic Spectrum: A Guide for Parents and Professionals.* London: Constable.

Articles available on my website (www.maxineaston.co.uk)

Aston, M.C. (2003) 'Asperger syndrome in the counselling room.' *Counselling and Psychotherapy Journal 14,* 5.

Aston, M.C. (2005) 'Growing up in an Asperger family.' *Counselling Children and Young People*, Summer.

Aston, M.C. (2007) 'Recognising AS and its implications for therapy.' BACP Information Sheet G9. Lutterworth: British Association for Counselling and Psychotherapy.

Aston. M.C. (2012) 'Asperger syndrome in the bedroom.' *Sexual and Relationship Therapy: International Perspectives on Theory, Research and Practice 27*, 1, 73–79.

Simons H.F. and Thompson, J.R. (2009) 'Affective deprivation disorder: does it constitute a relational disorder?' Available at www.maxineaston.co.uk/research/Affective%20Deprivation.pdf, accessed on 12 September 2013.

INDEX

acceptance of diagnosis 41–2
adolescents
    with Asperger syndrome 33–4
and parents with Asperger syndrome
    95–6
American Psychiatric Association (APA)
    18
anger
    arguments 119–20
    avoidance of 79, 83
    and depression 80
    displaced 120–1
    and domestic violence 118–19
    expression of 82–3, 119
    positive channelling 80–1
    and respect 81–2
    sensitivity to 79–80
    verbal abuse 121
arguments 119–20
Asperger, Hans 17, 19
Asperger syndrome (AS)
    and adolescence 33–4
    blaming 116–17
    diagnosis of 37–40
    gender difference 21–2, 24–6
    hereditary nature of 19–20
    increase in diagnosis 24–6
    lack of empathy 114–15
    lack of reciprocity 115–16
    as lifelong condition 33–4
    named 17
    nature of 27–8
    parenting 91–6
    prevalence of 20
    self-help for 125–6
    in social situations 32–3, 60–1,
        105–13
    special interests 99–101
    uniqueness of 59–60
    women undiagnosed 21–2, 24–6
Aspergirls (Simone) 22
assumptions in communication 71–2
Attwood, Tony 22, 23, 73, 91

Autism Spectrum Disorder (ASD)
    definition of 18
    gender difference
    triad of social and language
        impairments 18–19
    prevalence of 20
awareness before diagnosis 37–8

baby care 93
Bailey, A. 19
Baird, G. 20
Baron-Cohen, Simon 23, 48, 99
blaming 116–17
body language 36
Brugha, T.S. 20
bullying
    effect of 34
Burgoine, E. 18

Centers for Disease Control and
    Prevention (CDCP) 86
children
    and Asperger syndrome 33–4
    rules negotiation 94–5
common interests 49, 101
communication
    assumptions in 71–2
    awkwardness in 64–5
    body language 36
    complete messages 67–9
    difficulties with 62–3
    disclosure difficulties 66–7
    exaggerations in 107–8
    'I' usage 69–70
    importance of 63–4
    and intelligence 65–6
    and internet usage 75
    lights down during 75–6
    listening skills 76
    motivation for 74–5
    non-verbal 35–6, 63–4, 71–2
    and personal space 36
    problems with meanings 35
    responses in 70–1, 120–3